BEHIND
THE
MAGIC MIRROR

The Memoir of Romper Room's Miss Sandra

Sandra Hart

A Ballinswood Book
Published by Myartisanway Press
NEW JERSEY

Cover Art by Brett Thompson, copyright © 2002, myartisanway.com
Cover photo by Demetrius Constantinus

Library of Congress Control Number: 2002110097
ISBN 0-9715525-0-9

Published by
Myartisansway Press
P.O. Box 121
Navesink, New Jersey 07752
Ballinswoodbooks@aol.com
Myartisansway.com
Toll free 866-294-9063
Fax 732-291-4903

Printed in the United States of America
Published 2002

To My Children

My journey began before you came.
I didn't know part of the way
You were to walk with me.

I traveled unknowingly
Seeking roads along the way
Looking for that perfect life
An Eden where we could stay.

Sometimes the way was unclear.
We often journeyed in darkness
Misguided by my ignorance
Complicated by my innocence.

I have taken you places
You may never have been
Had destiny not chosen you
To travel along with me.

Your journey will take its own course
And as was meant to be
I will continue along my paths
Guided by choices yet unknown to me.

Take my hand and bid farewell
Our paths to touch now and then.
Each journey's day I feel blessed
It was meant to be, part of the way
You were to walk with me.

Acknowledgments

These are the composers who have provided the music to my words.

My husband, Arthur, my constant conductor.
My children, Brett, Alison and Emerson for their lyrical inspiration.
My grandchildren, Marshell and William who added the high notes.
My editor, Richard Maxson, who orchestrated the score.

I thank all of them for inspiring me to sing my song.

INTRODUCTION

It has taken me a long time to be able to be in the moment and to enjoy each day as it comes.

It seems that throughout my life, I have let my problems and outside interference overwhelm me so, that I have traveled each day missing the joys of my life; those joys that were tucked in between the events in my world that were causing chaos. And therefore, while writing this memoir, I realize that there is much that I have lost. I have lost the small joys of past living that I can never retrieve because I was so consumed with the negative forces in my life. I let those forces control me.

Growing up in Ohio I constantly wished the days away; waiting to be well, waiting to graduate; waiting to leave. Later on I was waiting to get discovered; waiting to get married; waiting to give birth; waiting for every dream I wanted to be fulfilled. Then finally, I waited and hoped to survive. And while I waited, yesterday died and tomorrow was not fully lived.

I have finally learned to be aware of here and now and to enjoy each moment of my day, but it has taken a long time for me to reach this point in my life, a point where I can be grateful for each and every minute. And on September 11, 2001 this lesson as a way of life hit very close to home.

The early morning sun was in full bloom and the air was apple clear and crisp as a September morning should be. My husband took his newspaper out to the deck and I puttered around the kitchen in slow motion, having had only four hours sleep because of an over-due writing assignment. By the time I settled in with my hot coffee at his side, my back to the warming sun, I ignored the beautiful ocean view as I poured more cream into my cup.

Our house sits on the highest point of the Atlantic shoreline and the glistening Sandy Hook Bay gives way to the dark rolling Atlantic beyond the beach. Rising above the ocean swells that God should have reasoned was enough beauty for us humans to savor at one time, and stretching as far as the eye can see, the crown jewels of the Northeast glistened as the new sun set fire to the windowed skyline of New York City. The ability to have this panorama in my life on a daily basis never bores me and I usually don't take it for granted. But that Tuesday was not a usual day.

The phone rang. Why so early, I mumbled to myself. My daughter was on the other end.

"Mother, an airplane slammed into the World Trade Center."

Her words were incredible. Did I hear her right? "What?" I said as I turned toward the ocean, my eyes searching to prove her wrong. I looked out onto the familiar horizon and billows of dark smoke were erasing the color from the blue sky that stretched along the rest of the city skyline and beyond.

My husband and I watched in disbelief, hardly grasping what we were seeing, when another large billow of smoke erupted like a white silk parachute exploding at full force and lifting vertically into the air.

Our neighbors started coming one by one and we gathered shoulder to shoulder on the deck, each of us silenced by the enormous spectacle. Then one by one they dispersed just as quietly as they came and Arthur and I went into the house to watch with the rest of the world the unfolding of the tragic events we just witnessed.

Six hours later I was back on the deck, still somewhat in shock and staring at unending clouds of death blowing with the afternoon winds northward, trailing high into the sky. The Magnificent Maidens who guarded our city of cities at the point where the ocean and rivers bleed into one another are gone.

Here I was in America, standing on the ocean's edge among the green trees with a gentle wind tousling my hair. In this bucolic setting I was watching a war 14 miles away. It was more surreal than anything I could have even imagined I would ever witness. It was unthinkable. It was unbelievable. Only the steady groan of the large ferries traveling back and forth executing rescue missions between our two shores kept me in reality. This was not just a bad dream. Who would have thought it could happen here?

The smoke was still there the next day across the water, hanging heavily to the ground by the morning wind, but reality unfolded several days later when the smoke cleared and the familiar nightlights revealed an empty place in the sky.

The memory of what I saw that Tuesday from our eagle's nest is a part of me forever.

I am old enough to remember listening to the radio while cross-legged on the floor when President Franklin Roosevelt died. I was too young to understand the sadness our country felt, but I remember. I remember that I was feeding my baby when television news told us that John F. Kennedy had been shot and I cried.

And when Martin Luther King was assassinated I was both saddened and fearful.

I will remember that day. I will remember how we here in America died as a result of unspeakable acts of violence against innocent people. Those who lost their lives in these tragic terrorist attacks are gone forever. Those of us that have been left behind have lost something that next to life is precious as well.

We have lost our ability to feel safe from terrorism in any corner of America. We have lost an important part of our freedom.

I will never forget where I was on that horrendous day when deeds of man against man were applauded in the name of religion. I will never again take for granted every minute of each day I have been given. What I have lost in my past, I will fill with my future one day at a time.

I dedicate my story to all that have loved

To all who have suffered

To all who have searched for the truth

I dedicate this to my children and my husband

To all whom I have loved

I dedicate this to the memory of Jennings Lee Hart

1929 -1980

1

Houses. When I think back on my life the memories that are filed away in that part of my mind seem to be directly related to the places I have lived and what happened within their rooms. Somehow I seem to remember more about those houses and what happened within them in more detail than some events in my life. Even today, where I live and my environment have a profound effect on how I feel. When I have been able to choose my surroundings, the places where I have been happy have been bright and the windows uncovered to let the light stream in. The other houses in my past that were dark, those I have lived in as a child, or when others had control over my life, remain in my mind as representing a dismal place in my existence.

I grew up in a steel town that long before my family arrived was given breath by the industrial revolution and had risen like the Phoenix from the banks of the Ohio River Valley. The hillside homes looked to me like matchboxes stuck in uneven rows reaching down to the water's edge. Sometimes as I rode along in my father's old Model-T, I would press my face against its window and look up and squint my eyes to blur the images. I imagined them to be hungry ravens on the rocky cliffs, perched and ready to fly down and sweep me away under the darkness of their wings. I could easily imagine that darkness because shadows and smoke the same lifeless color of the metal produced in the mills along the river covered the houses on the inside and out with a darkness that never left. A darkness that in spite of the prosperity from the mills stayed with those that lived inside the houses, too.

The steel mill's vast furnaces devoured tons of coal around the clock and belched continuous white-hot fire from beneath the dripping vats of molten metal that once expelled, spewed like vomit into waiting troughs to cool. It was the thick acrid smoke from the coal that was to be blamed for the constant shadows in which we lived, the gauze that draped Steubenville in monochromatic tones of gray. Even then as a young child I wished to escape to the sun of my grandfather's farm again. But for most of the grownups the smoke and fire polluting the air could just as easily have been God spitting gold from the bowels of the chimney stacks as far as they were concerned. The country was hungry for steel and there was work for everyone who was lucky enough to pass through the high, galvanized gates with a union card.

It was 1948 and World War II was over and the world was changing. Urban migration escalated and Steubenville continued to grow. People were leaving the farms in the outlying areas of the valley to cash in on the union wages and the good life the local mills provided. Our family was one of them. For Steubenville's immigrants, mostly of European descent, the mills represented freedom and prosperity; their dreams come true. For people like my father, American of English decent and whose ancestors came ashore generations ago, it was steady work and a house to rent and new clothes and long needed visits to the dentist for their children. For all of them it was a new beginning after the war.

In our house on Saturdays the smell of pine and ammonia hung heavily about our heads and made my nostrils sting as I helped my mother attempt to wash away from the windows and floor the dark gritty covering that somehow got through our tightly sealed house. Useless work to dress these wooden boxes with rooms to live in, my mother would say. To me also, the job seemed endless and mostly hopeless, as week in and week out we set about to erase the traces of the outside world that intruded into our lives and landed on Mother's belongings. I now know they were the only symbols of any dignity she perceived she had left since Daddy had taken work in the mill.

I remember that yellow box of a house, its long front porch and the cement steps neatly cutting through the walled bank of sloping grass that lead to the sidewalk below. The entryway with steps on the left climbing to three bedrooms and leading to the musty basement where the wringer washer ca-chugged and long rope lines for the wash zigzagged across the length of the cement floor that never seemed to dry.

The living room was right off the entry and a curved archway invited visitors into another room made for dining but used by us as the place we really escaped, all the chairs placed for easy viewing and centered around our 19" RCA floor model television. Since the arrival of the magic black and white test patterned world came into our living room, a world beyond the life we knew in Steubenville, the days of lingering in the kitchen listening to "The Green Hornet" and "Dick Tracy" on our tube radio after dinner were gone.

In spite of Mother's sighs of yesterday's life and her dreams of something better someday, she was temporarily resigned to her fate and not the least impressed with our new RCA in its ugly square case and blank face gazing out upon her good stuff. She lovingly decorated her pretend palace with her antiques and homemade drapes and ideas she copied from Good Housekeeping Magazine.

The centerpiece of her kitchen was her handcrafted oilcloth wall-hanging in the kitchen portraying two Dutch children in white starched hats with yellow wooden clogs standing by a wheelbarrow full of brightly colored tulips that she displayed with pride. Those children, that boy and girl, staring down at me every moment I spent in the kitchen eating, playing or doing my homework, after awhile became real to me. It was as though they, too, were a part of my family, watching us eat Mother's meals of overcooked calves' liver and beef stew or on Fridays, bony fried fish. And they kept me company on the long winter nights as I struggled with my math homework. But they were, as everything in our house, not permanent and could easily travel, taken down from the wall and packed into the moving van that would take us away from 1414 Pennsylvania Avenue. Someday.

But as time continued to pass our house on Pennsylvania eventually was no longer thought or spoken of as a short stopover by Mother. It became her home and no longer just a house. She slowly talked less and less about our big house in Washington, D. C. on Eleventh Street where my brother Sherman and I were born. It is where we had lived with hired help to care for us; with its high-ceiling rooms with beautiful paintings and tennis courts out back and, of course, with Daddy's drinking that caused us to lose it all.

I was just about five when we left Washington so I have limited memories of my life there, but Mother said I had been delivered very quickly into her world kicking and screaming on a cold Sunday night exactly one week after the New Year. My best guess is that my homecoming was less than spectacular since I was laid in a dresser drawer lined with a wool blanket and placed on the cherry wood bed in my parent's room. Why there was no bassinet waiting for my arrival, I was never told. My parents were certainly people who could afford better, but perhaps the presence of my father's strong-willed mother who ruled the house deemed that the need for such foolishness as a cradle or such nonsense was a waste since a drawer would do just fine. My brother who was three at the time proclaimed with wonder that this new thing intruding into his life had eyes and a nose and could we give it away to Miranda, his nanny.

I do remember my Aunt Mabel, Mother's oldest sister, with her hard-felt hugs, red nail polish and smells of perfume. An afternoon with my aunt was always something to remember. Mabel was the only one of my grandparent's ten children that wanted to be an actress. Grandpa, who had made money in the coal industry, was considered a rich man at the time, so he sent her to drama school. But before she could do much with her lessons, she fell in love with her dentist and got married and moved from Ohio to Washington, D.C. where he opened a new practice. That kind of ended any aspirations she had for the theater. Her husband, Doc, drank and then she started drinking. Whether it was from regret seeing her dreams evaporate, who knows, but she and Doc had two children that were grown up and by the time I came along she and Doc were alone with their Scotch in their big dark house.

Aunt Mabel would let me dress up in her fox wrap that had the head and glass eyes still attached. It had a clip under the fox's mouth that would grab on to his tail after she wrapped it around my shoulders. I had to hold my chin up high while she wrapped it around twice to keep it from falling off. Then Mabel would press me to her bosoms in a hug and lift me onto her dressing room table stool so that I could see myself in the mirror. "You look so lovely, Miss. Where are you going tonight?" she would say and she made me feel beautiful.

Once I remember her painting my nails and my promising her that I wouldn't show them to Daddy. But I was so pleased with myself and thought they were amazingly beautiful that when my father came to pick me up, my crimson nails were the first things I showed him.

Daddy's fury at her for daring to guild his innocent little lily with her wicked red polish, "the color of loose women" was not what I had expected. I hated him for being so mean to my aunt and I was afraid she was angry with me for not doing what she had told me to do. With me in tow, Daddy left in a huff and I can't remember that I was ever allowed to go visit Aunt Mabel again alone.

I remember Sunday afternoons at double features with my family and dinner at the Lotus where grownups danced to live music. I remember roller skating with Sherman and holding onto the high iron fence around our house to keep from falling. I remember the men in soldier's clothes sitting in the lobby of the Willard Hotel and the runny red-colored liver Mother bought at the corner butcher store to feed to the turtle at my brother's kindergarten. The school that seemed so far away across the dusty circled park with its tall trees and gray squirrels that circled our feet looking for a handout.

I don't remember the Easter Egg Rolls on the White House lawn or the cherry blossoms, or visiting the zoo. But I'll never forget the loneliness I felt when I heard the grownup's talking about the tragic death of my Aunt Mabel from a fall down her basement stairs just before we moved to Ohio. She was my very first best friend and I missed her hugs and fancy smells and red nail polish for a long time.

Several years ago I had the lead as Catherine the Great in an off-Broadway play. My costume came from the archives of the Metropolitan Opera and helped make it easier for me to physically construct and become the character I was portraying. The gown was of exquisite brocade with a fitted waist and flowing back. Just imagining what diva may have worn the costume on the great stage at the Met before me increased its power of grandness that made me feel Catherine's greatness. In the dressing room before my first performance, in costume and running lines back at myself in the mirror to warm up and take the edge off my nerves, the reflection I saw was quite curious. It was my Aunt Mabel looking back at me.

The only memento left to me of Aunt Mabel is a picture of her in theatrical costume. Now in my mirror, there she stood. I never had been aware of it before, but within the character of an older Queen Catherine I had physically become my Aunt Mabel as she was in my photograph of her. I'd like to think that maybe her lusty spirit was there inside of Catherine, finally walking the boards she so loved and left behind when she married Uncle Doc.

2

Every corner of my bedroom in our house on Pennsylvania Avenue with it's second story window overlooking the long fenced-in backyard extending to the alley beyond is etched permanently in my mind. From its windows when I was twelve I watched the leaves turn green to brown and then fall and sail from the trees. I watched the snow cover the oxygen-starved grass. I watched the forsythia and pussy willows bloom in the spring and watched our crazy German Shepherd, BJ, dig out the tulip bulbs as fast as my mother could plant them. After enough doing and then redoing she finally gave up on the garden and concentrated on her interior decorating. This proved to be a safer haven away from BJ and his love for mining the yard and undermining Mother's work.

I still remember every inch of the patterned wallpaper with its tiny faded pink and blue flowers dancing along the walls and my worn stack of comic books under the other window that looked out onto the house next door. In that room within a course of a year, I celebrated my thirteenth birthday, got my first period, my first pimple, and shaved under my arms for the first time.

I was confined to my bed for six months in the spring of that memorable year after suffering through several bouts of strep throat. At the top of the stairs, in the corner bedroom where my double bed angled squarely into the far recess of the space, and when house calls from a family doctor were expected, I was diagnosed with rheumatic fever. I was ordered to stay there until the illness had run its cycle.

I should have thought it a fate worse than death, this pronouncement that I had to stay in bed for who knows how long. But at twelve, I had no sense of the time involved in recovery, or caution about rheumatic fever and its possible serious side effects, including death and severe heart damage.

The first few weeks, I experienced an initial sense of drama, maybe even a little excitement about being sick. At least it was a way out of the Saturday scrubbing. Whatever it was I was thinking, I know it made me feel special or different in some way. But it did not take long for the drama of being ill and the center of attention to begin to wear thin.

At first the news of my illness captured my friends' imaginations and they came around often and sat on my bed as we gossiped about the boys we had crushes on, but soon they quit coming around. Maybe they thought I would make them sick, but more than anything it was probably just that it was boring for them. After all, I didn't really have a life anymore that they could identify with now that I was bedridden.

I soon began to feel the isolation from the active world I had known and the knowledge that the stigma of being sick and different and maybe, even contagious, brought an overwhelming sense of loneliness and insecurity into my life. The pink penicillin liquid spooned to me by my mother was no longer fun to take. I wanted to turn the clock back and start all over again. I was sick and tired of being sick. Why should I be locked away in my bedroom prison while the rest of my friends were having a good time? Perhaps if I closed my eyes I would wake up and it would be only a dream. I wanted to close my eyes and make everything go away. But it didn't.

I don't know how many weeks it took for me to quit feeling sorry for myself, but after awhile, having no other alternatives, I resigned to make a world within the confines of my wallpapered room. Daddy brought up an old round-shouldered wooden radio and plugged it in near my bed. His doing so opened up a whole world to me -- soap operas and radio news. All of the characters in One Man's Family and Ma Perkins became my friends. BJ would curl up at the bottom of my bed exhausted from digging and without a care in the world, licking his privates. And I would spend hours listening to the woes and loves of my new daily radio friends and wonder at news stories of far away places like Korea where there was a war going on. My radio was a major part of my survival through the long days of recovery and I can still see in my mind the soul of my electronic friend, at night the soft orange lights of its tubes as they illuminated my room and kept me company.

At my mother's suggestion to help pass the time, I read the Bible from cover to cover. One day I was immersed in my reading. And I can't recall what chapter or verse it was since it was the only beginning to end reading I have done, but what I read more or less told me I would be damned forever if I used the Lord's name in vain. When my twelve year old brain computed those words a shock went through me and I vowed in fear never to utter anything close to a curse that would put me on the side of the Devil and land me in Hell. I wanted out of bed and dared not even think of anything that would keep me there one day longer than necessary. After I read what could happen to me, I prayed every night that the temptation would never come upon me to lose my place in heaven so foolishly by taking the Lord's name in vain. But as much as I tried to get even the quickest thought of those words that would bring damnation down on my head out of my mind, they would slip back again with a force I knew must be inspired by Satan himself. Just like being afraid of looking out of the window because you might jump. It was the same thing for me and I was so afraid that I would outright say a curse word because it just was there. And, of course, I knew I would be doomed. I even planned that if the temptation came I would just put my pillow over my head to muffle my words so not even God could hear. But my will power held and that temptation eventually passed. I assured myself that if I could withstand the temptation the Devil had placed before me, then I had the courage and will power to overcome anything, even rheumatic fever.

When I was in the depth of my illness, Daddy's friend from Washington who Sherman and I called Uncle Charlie made a special visit just to see me. Uncle Charlie was a cousin of Winston Churchill and he looked so much like his famous relative that they could have been twins. Sitting back, lighting up a fat cigar, and after much begging on our part, he would always entertain us with exciting stories of his and Winston's mischievous boyhood adventures together.

One of my favorites that we made him tell us over and over again was the time young Winston was visiting Charles during a summer holiday. Having tired of playing soldiers in the yard, Winston and Charlie found some firecrackers hidden in a pantry drawer and decided to surprise Uncle Charlie's Mama during her afternoon nap by gently rolling a lighted fire cracker under her bed. They quietly tiptoed up the staircase and crouching on their hands and knees, pushed open Mama's door and Winston, with his best aim, let the missile tumble and land under its target. The boys barely had a chance to stand upright before the sharp crack echoed from the room, followed by Mama's scream and a blood-curdling yowl. Lady Carabantas, the family cat, who had been napping under the bed, her hair standing on end and smoking, what little was left, came flying out like a bullet between Charlie's legs, knocking him off balance. Together Lady Carabantas and Charlie rolled down the stairs, claws and legs entwined while Winston headed for the back stairs, out of sight. Well, the next thing they knew, Winston was summoned home to England and Charlie was left alone to nurse his wounds and suffer the wrath of his parents and Lady Carabantas. His mother's famous quote that big Uncle Charlie would always mimic in a falsetto voice made us giggle, 'What a pity! That Churchill boy will never amount to anything!' Then Uncle Charlie would laugh and laugh with us, his fat belly jiggling underneath his suit jacket.

Mother never told me until years later when Uncle Charlie died that at the time of his visit with me, he told her that he feared I would not make it though my illness. He was always so cheerful when he came, I had no idea of his great concern about the gravity of my condition. He never had any children of his own and I believe that he loved my brother and I as though we were really his very own family.

Although she had come to accept her life in Steubenville, perhaps my mother's earlier dreams of escaping her fate in our little house and the dreary life revolving around us there subconsciously propelled me to dream of getting away someday. I thought about it constantly during the long months of my illness, the drama eventually losing out to the painful reality as the days droned on. But whatever the reason, maybe I was just born to fly, from the beginning I never felt that Steubenville or Pennsylvania Avenue was my home or that I really belonged there. I always felt a longing for another life somewhere and I yearned of the day when I could escape the prison walls the beak rocky cliffs represented to me. I longed to spread my wings and fly away, far away to the life that I saw on television and the movies. I had a fire burning within me that the confinement of my illness fanned and no one could extinguish. I had dreams to be fulfilled that I would not let die. In that respect I was not my mother's daughter. I would accept nothing less than making my dreams a reality. I had to get better.

Not that it was Mother's fault that her dreams never were realized. It's just that her choices in her youth and the restrictions on women and their ambitions in her day were much more limiting. She, too, had been sickly as a child. Typhoid fever struck her when she was quite little and they shaved her head down to her scalp. There were nine other children to care for, but being sickly and considered the weak one, both Grandma and Grandpa and even her older brothers and sisters catered to "poor little Verta". She got so used to this preferred treatment that it was hard to recognize that the world outside her family would not always feel that way.

Grandpa had lost most of his wealth when Mother was seventeen so there was no money for beautiful clothes unless she earned it herself. She went to live with Mabel and for a short time she was a model at the Woodard and Lothrup department store in Washington. She was very beautiful then and remained so, even into her nineties, but she never let go of wanting to be the center of attention. The best thing that anyone could say to her when she was in her prime was that she was attractive, and later when she was in her nineties, that she didn't look it.

Mother was very creative and smart I think, but I don't remember her reading anything other than magazines or a newspaper. Her curiosity did not seem to range beyond her home and the people she loved. She traveled very little. Looking back, I am to think that her life was her possessions that included both animate and inanimate, her things and her family, but not necessarily in that order. That was all that mattered.

She and my father met in Doc's dental office and they married before the war started and she retired to assume what she thought her new role should be; caretaker of all that she loved. And that was her life and the way she lived it to the end. She died at the age of ninety-one putting on lipstick for a visit to her children.

Although he was a constant in my life, my father in those early years is woven through the eyes of my mother more than from the fabric of what I can remember.

What stands out in my mind is his prickly mustache tickling my cheek when he kissed me good night and how warm and safe I felt as he held and sang me to sleep. And that his voice that seemed to come from a place so distant made sleep come easily and peacefully. I thought he was beautiful like my mother.

Daddy always rose before dawn to go to the mill and was tired and went to bed early when he came home. When he worked the night shift he came home too late for us to still be awake. On his days off, he would dress up and go downtown for the day. I hardly ever saw him. Maybe that's why my recall of his participation in my early life is so unclear.

It was on Daddy's late nights when Sherman and I would be sleeping that I do remember being awakened by the angry voices of my parents down in the kitchen, and my fear of the voices, but all the rest, if anything, I have shut out from my memories. That is, with the exception on one night when I was about six. In the darkness I was frightened at hearing my parents yell at each other and then I heard the front door open and slam closed. Sherman got out of bed first and I followed him to the window. I was too small to peek out over the window ledge into the darkness, even on my tiptoes, but Sherman said he saw our mother walking away from the house. I was so afraid that she was leaving us and would never come back. I went to my bed and crawled under the cold covers so scared my body shook all night. I listened a long time for the door to open, but it didn't and sometime during the night my brother and I fell asleep. Mother was home by the time we awakened and neither my brother nor I ever let on we heard anything.

As I got older my father used to say that I wore my heart on my sleeve. And as much as it hurt my feelings when he said that to me, his truth not only wounded me, but also convinced me his all-knowing parental perception of his daughter was precisely on the mark. Being as sensitive as I was, the last thing I needed was for my father to point out how imperfect and vulnerable I was. He never forgot to remind me I was suffering from being too sensitive for this world.

The seed planted as to what I was through my father's eyes grew and after I was well enough to back to school my life did not resume where it left off before I got sick. All of my self-confidence I had gotten from my earlier will power experience and my Bible reading quickly left me. My friends sort of had gotten used to being without me and it was as though I was the new girl in town all over again and I had to earn a space within the group everyone wanted to be with. Some thought that rheumatic fever was catching, so they stayed away. I had gained weight during my inactive bed existence and I was wearing braces on my teeth when I went back to school.

To make matters worse, I had to leave my classes early because I had to climb the stairs one by one slowly and needed extra time to get from one class to another. The humiliation of having to leave class knowing that the others would be running up the steps past me when the bell rang to get to the next class while I was still plodding along, forced me to keep my eyes focused only on the steps ahead of me. As hard as I tried, I never really fit in again with my old friends who were part of the "in crowd". These factors, impacted to a great extent by the stigma of being "the sick girl", withdrew me further within myself. I found what satisfaction could be had under the circumstances by building my high school life around academic achievements. The lowest point in my teenage life came when I was a junior in high school. I was the only girl to decorate the gym for the prom to go home and not return for the dance. No one had asked me to my own party.

It was this final isolation beyond my bedroom that drove me to bury myself further into my studies and plan even more fervently of leaving Steubenville for good. I couldn't wait to graduate and as in my fantasies, fly away to a better place, a better life. And I was only sixteen.

3

I can't define a point in time, the age I was, or when I first understood that my father was an alcoholic. I remember his anger and the beatings with his belt on our bottoms when Sherman and I had disobeyed Mother, but I don't recall when I began to associate my father's anger with his drinking. I just know that my brother and I were like little puppies, learning with a few early experiences with Daddy's leather belt that it could be used on us on those nights he came home trailing 'the strong smell' about the house.

Sherman and I would lie in our beds shaking when Daddy came home late in fear of his heavy footsteps on the stairs. It was always a sigh of relief when his uneven gait passed our door and he stumbled through another. We never knew why Mother felt her verbal punishments were not enough misery for us, and why she had to betray our childish misdeeds to our father, especially knowing the consequences that would befall her children.

Sherman was very stoic and never uttered a whimper as the sharp cracks sounded one after another against his backside. And not even my tears that I hoped would save me from my brother's fate would stop Daddy's stinging lashes. Using a hairbrush or belt to get your point across was not thought of as abusive in the 40's, but that didn't make it right or tolerable, or my father a child abuser. In those days, most children got whipped for misdeeds. Even in school, children were sent to the principals' office where their punishment would be meted out with a big wooden paddle.

Two things we could count on when Daddy was drinking. The belt and the sobering day after when he would give us surprises as tokens of atonement for his sins. When I was younger, to forgive him the welts on my behind, it was a coloring book and crayons.

Although the whippings stopped sometime before I was seven or eight, as I got older, I learned the power of my 'morning after' shunning. I wouldn't talk to him for days. It was my adolescent way of dealing with the hurt and disappointment I felt toward his drinking. I knew no other weapon to use against him and his behavior. I hated the screaming that went on between my parents because of Daddy's alcohol, and silence was my refuge, the place I could go within myself to make the discord, the drinking, the unhappiness all go away.

Then a miracle happened. When my grandma died while we were living on the farm, Daddy stopped drinking. I don't know whether it was his watching my mother's suffering at her overwhelming loss, or whether by having to live with his in-laws, he finally saw his reflection at the bottom of the well. What he thought, what made him quit 'cold turkey' he never shared with anyone, not even my mother. I just know that from that point on Daddy came alive again, and within a year we were heading up the road in the first car we owned since the war was over.

Daddy had found an old Model-T that he bought from a farmer who had it parked near his barn with a 'For Sale' sign on it. It must have been really old, because it didn't look like any of the other cars on the road when Sherman and I took the weekly grocery trips with our parents to the A&P store in Steubenville. Each trip we eagerly jumped up on the running board and slid across the worn leather seats in anticipation of our journey into town. My father would crank her up, and we would chug, chug along, peering out the small back windows, knowing that we were very rich, because our daddy had a car.

It wasn't too long after Daddy's sobriety and the Model-T, that Daddy got the union job at the steel mill in town. We moved from Grandpa's farm, leaving my innocent and idyllic existence in the dust as we drove up the dirt road to the main highway that would take us to Steubenville.

Nothing is forever. Unfortunately, not even my father's sobriety. It was Christmas Eve, just before my thirteenth birthday, and we were waiting for Daddy to come home for dinner. Well, he came home all right, and the old familiar smell recoiled my senses as he bent to kiss my cheek. I excused myself from the table and went to my room and cried into my pillow. I thought my heart would break, because I really loved my father and needed the security of knowing the anger the alcohol produced would not return into our lives.

The next morning Daddy's Christmas gift to me was an Emerson stereophonic phonograph player and records by my favorite singers; Eddie Fisher, the Four Aces and Frankie Lane. My gift to him was to finally let him know what his drinking did to me and how I hated the father who came home drunk. Mother and Sherman sat there by the Christmas tree, not moving, their eyes frozen on the lights smothered in angel hair that made halos of rainbows around the bulbs. Daddy just sat there in his plaid bathrobe, hanging his head down, looking at the floor. I was too big now for his belt, what else could he do to me?

Daddy never responded to my venting. He just got up and walked into the kitchen. I heard the oven door squeak open, then close, smelled the escaping aroma of roasting turkey drift into the room, and that was it. He went upstairs to take a nap before dinner and he never took a drink again for the rest of his ninety-two years. That was the best Christmas gift I have ever received.

My children have since confessed to me that the punishment that I handed out that was the worst and most hurtful, was when I would quit talking. This revelation from my children took me by surprise, because I never realized that I ever did that with any of them. But there it was, laid out for me, so I had to believe that I *did* do it.

As I have remembered childhood hurts, so do my children. And it was not until I started thinking about my life and my relationship with my father, that I understood my habits with my own children. As I did with Daddy, I was trying to change their behavior by hiding my own hurts and disappointments with my silence. It was a survival pattern I developed as a child that, unfortunately, I carried it on through my relationship with my children without even knowing it.

4

A few years ago on a visit to Ohio I returned to Grandpa's house that stood at the heart of the fork in the road leading from Bloomingdale. On the spot where my grandparent's farm house was, I found only mounds of broken earth seemingly disconnected, then filled in again; the tell tale scars of strip mining. Where once stood our old house, only scars of earth overgrown with weeds remained. I walked the property along the edge of the road and reminded myself that some memories are best laid to rest after they have been lived; remain where they have slept as a note of happier times. Conceivably, it would have been better to have not come at all. I thought it ironic, that since Grandpa was the first to bring strip mining to this part of the country, that in the end, his house had been swallowed up by the monster he created.

Grandpa only went as far as the second grade, but he was never one to let the grass grow beneath his feet. He probably was wheeling and dealing before the school door closed behind him.

From what I know, when he was big enough to pull a cart, he earned a living by peddling produce at the back doors of the wealthy homes in the area. Eventually, that's how he met my grandmother. She worked as a domestic in one of those big houses, and from the way he used to tell it, "The minute Mammy opened the back door and I saw her, I never wanted anyone else." So lucky Grandpa married the beautiful Pennsylvania Dutch girl with dark hair and rosy cheeks who had stolen his heart, and whisked her, a young girl with modest wants, away into the whirlwind of his life.

Grandpa went from peddling to eventually owning his own produce store and then to buying up farms and selling the coal rights to the stripping companies. In time, his business dealings gave him great wealth and he shared it with the community by building churches. He shared with his family by giving his grown sons airplanes and fancy cars, his daughters beautiful clothes and his wife, an interior decorator to furnish their house with fine furniture and velvet drapes.

But as the wheel so often turns, through the years, his business savvy finally betrayed him and he more or less wound up where he started. And the whirlwind in which Grandma was helplessly twirling, finally dropped her to the ground at a time when she should have had better.

Three of her daughters with their husbands and children had returned to the nest to get their lives together after the war, including us. My grandmother was ill when we moved to the farm. After a life with Grandpa; several early miscarriages; cooking and sewing for the 10 remaining children; living in luxury and then having it taken away at a time she could have enjoyed it, her energy was spent. The poor woman, now depleted of her strength, had the responsibility of a full house back in her lap.

No matter how temporary our intended stays were, as I think back on it now, I am inclined to believe that this final burden was the end of my grandma.

For the young cousins it was paradise; playing hide-and-seek in the cornfields; stealing strawberries from the garden and looking for frogs in the dank springhouse. The big pines in the front yard that were painted around the trunks with white wash were great hiding places when our parents were calling us to fill the buckets for drinking and bathing water from the pump outside the back kitchen door. The rest of the town up the road had the luxury of indoor plumbing, but we scrambled at night and in the morning to be first in line at the 'two-seater' outhouse. I always wondered 'why' the extra seat - who would want company in there? It was worth our while to get up with the roosters, otherwise, emergencies had to be covered by the smelly chamber pots in each room. Just having to lift the lid on a full pot was punishment in itself for sleeping in.

Throwing stones for Pete to chase, my grandparent's German Shepherd, was at least an hour's worth of fun each day. His furry flesh rippling, set in motion by the force of his powerful muscles on every stride and final pounce, he would eagerly capture the stone in his mighty jaws, and after returning, drop it proudly at our feet. His tongue hanging loosely and dripping with saliva, his big brown eyes and furrowed brow always begged for another throw. He wasn't particular, it was the game that mattered. Pete would even play fetch with old smelly cans we would find in the garbage pile behind the outhouse. He would dent them with his strong jaws until they were almost flat. The same with stones. He would start with a big one and by the end of a week's worth of chasing and chewing, the stones would be slimy and chiseled down to practically nothing. Just like his teeth.

Then after we wore old Pete out and left him to limp off to digest or chew whatever we had been tossing, we would go racing barefoot through the morning dew to see who could be first to reach the rope hammock anchored by gigantic rusty hooks between two fir trees in the side yard.

Once in a clever trick (I told him he had a hole in the back of his britches) I out maneuvered my cousin, Brad, and got there first. He was so mad, he flipped me out of the hammock and I landed on my stomach knocking the breath out of me. I thought it surely was the end, because I couldn't get my lungs to work for what seemed like forever. Brad got a spanking from Grandpa, and just for spite, even though I was finished with the hammock, I swung for a long tiresome time to keep him from getting it.

Looking back, I think the only times we weren't fighting for lazing in the hammock, were the days when the thrashers were coming to cut the down the fields and bale the hay. The loud 'th-rush th-rush' of the big paddle wheel behind the machine was music to our ears as it ate its way, back and forth, back and forth in neat rows through the fields. The harvested hay then would be shaped into square bales, bound with wire and loaded onto wagons to take to the barn. Usually Grandpa would let us hitch a ride on the last wagonload and we scrambled for places atop the pungent smelling bales; seeds and loose pieces of hay sticking to our hair and in the cuffs of our overalls. Sometimes we even dragged Pete aboard, slobber and all, as the tractor pulled away with us in tow.

Naturally, being as young as I was, I never thought about why so many of us were visiting our grandparents at the same time, but as heavenly as it was for us children to have built- in playmates, it must have been far from heaven for our parents. Being there meant they had fallen on hard times; little money, no work and no where else to go.

But for Grandma, who had already paid her dues as a caretaker, it must have been even worse. Afflicted with angina, her arteries clogged from her fatty good cooking, she died before the last family had gotten on their feet and left the nest. She never lived to reclaim her house.

My grandma died on Christmas Eve that year and it was the worst Christmas I've ever had in my life. Christmas morning when I saw Grandma's overnight case that a few days earlier I had carefully helped my mother pack to take to Grandma in the hospital hidden under the breakfront near the Christmas tree, I knew she was never coming home. No one had to tell me. I knew with great sadness in my young heart. I knew.

So, that meant for me, by the time I was eight, I had lost two special people. But as the circle of life rotated, it brought me something else; the love of words. I discovered my love of books and the words within them during my stay on the farm. My mother's childhood book, the only one I have known her to have, "Alice All Alone"; the complete works of Charles Dickens, gilded-edged-leather-bound editions that came to us from my father's family; Bible stories left by Jehovah Witnesses traveling the back country roads, spreading the Word. They became my playmates. My eyes consumed each wondrous page and took me on exciting adventures that, in my mind, became alive to me.

Tiny Tim and his family and all of Mr. Dickens' characters became a part of my life. In Mother's book, I felt sorry for poor, lonely Alice and wished she lived near me because I would be her friend. These first books were the beginning of a lifelong thirst for words, their power and the magic they possess.

After working on this chapter and writing about my first experiences of discovering my love for books, those memories reawakened a longing for my old beloved books. As a result, I took time away from my computer to rearrange the attic in search of them.

I went about my task with childlike enthusiasm, peering and poking about inside dark boxes, until I remembered that a friend's daughter once reached into a dark drawer and got bitten by a recluse spider. The spider's toxic bite caused her to lose part of her hand.

So, resuming my search with much more cautious digging about that summer's day up in our beastly hot attic, I finally found what I was searching for. I found my treasured books among Mother's boxes that had been transferred to our attic after her death. Knowing that

Mother saved anything and everything that belonged to her children, her way did not disappoint me.

I transported the dusty box down the narrow stairs with great care and slid them one by one on the lower shelves in the library within easy reach of my grandchildren. After almost half a century lying silently between their yellowed pages, each of my treasured adventures can come alive again through my grandchildren's imaginations.

My thoughts of the transition time we spent on the Bloomingdale farm are cherished as part of the good times in my childhood. I can't ride through the countryside today without it bringing back the sense memory of the earthy smells of the hay and life on that farm, and when I think of what we and our parents had or didn't have at that time in our lives - we had it all.

If life and our raison d'être is finding our place while we are here, then in our move to Steubenville, I lost my place. The clock stopped ticking for me during those years. A friend of mine, after reading the unedited first couple of chapters in this memoir said to me, "Surely you weren't as unhappy as all that. There must be some good things that happened to you between eleven and eighteen? Somehow, I never thought it in your nature to be so negative." And I had to think about that, that maybe because I was so young, my recall had emphasized all the disappointments in my life during that time and I had shut the door on the others. Maybe my memories of that period have been, for years, so locked in place through a child's perspective, it was just convenient to leave them that way. I was slightly embarrassed at his suggestion that I might be closing off a part of my young life as it was, but I knew he was right. Just because the bad times seem to overshadow the good, there had to be fleetingly pleasant and important milestones somewhere within that mass of time.

For one, when Daddy quit drinking and he was around more, it changed our lives. Our household became somewhat normal, if there is such a thing. Then, in two unrelated incidences, there were the times I saved the lives of my friend Hannah and a baby I didn't know. The first one was when my friend and I went to the lake for a swim and she just disappeared under the water and didn't come back up. I dived under the murky water and grabbed her by her long pigtails that were floating freely like two loose ropes and pulled her to the surface. I was about eleven at the time. Then, when I was 18, I saved a baby who fell into the pool during my job as the lifeguard at the Steubenville Country Club. I made a flying leap from my high stand to reach her tiny body as it bobbled in the water. I got her out and although she was crying, she wasn't hurt, but her mother never thanked me. She just grabbed her wet, crying baby out of my arms and walked away. At the time, I wondered how anyone could be so ungrateful and I was rather put out about her slight, but now I realize that she was probably embarrassed that she hadn't been watching her child.

And if you had asked me, at eighteen, to list in order of importance the highs in my life, these would have been at the top of the list. First, in my senior year I finally had a boyfriend and got to go to my prom. Then was editor-in-chief of The Beacon, the high school newspaper, and received honors for my journalism achievements at graduation. But best of all was that I got accepted to a college out of state, away from all that represented oppression for me.

Although I was a good candidate for a scholarship to an Ivy League college, graduating with honors at the top part of my class, without parental guidance I was more or less left to my own devices to find a school. So I thought it would be sensible to apply to the University of Maryland to get back to Washington, D.C., the town in which I began my life. And indicating where my immature head was at the time, I also had applied to the University of Hawaii at the last minute, after I had listened to an LP flowing with Hawaiian music that filled my mind with fantasies of studying among the flowers and palm trees. I would have done almost anything to get away from Steubenville - and Hawaii was far! My acceptance to U of H came as the last suitcase was packed for Maryland, so perhaps luck was beginning to smile down on me. It was too late to even reconsider Hawaii, so I went to Maryland.

I left home that fall following graduation and said what I hoped would be my final adieu to Steubenville, my boyfriend, my childhood friends and the dreadful dark hills of the Ohio Valley. My parents drove me to the Pittsburgh Airport and as I took to the air, I watched the images of my mother and father on the observation deck below me become smaller and smaller and then disappear as though they were dots on the landscape. I turned away from the window and settled back in my seat. I knew my life in Steubenville would be just a memory. I wouldn't be back. I had been a stranger passing through.

5

The Asian flu. I arrived on campus in late August for freshman orientation and the big bug arrived not long after me in late fall. The oriental scourge was running rampant across the country. It hit Maryland with a vengeance and made most of us so ill that we crawled in droves to the infirmary to rid our weak and fevered bodies of this virus that was having breakfast, lunch and dinner on our immune systems.

I hadn't been this sick since I had my first and last experience with alcohol. Maryland was a dry campus, which meant no drinking on campus, so the students resorted to drinking vile brew made in secret by the chemistry students in the labs. The mystery concoction would then be poured into garbage cans big enough to last an evening of partying. The chaperons were usually alcoholics, so everyone felt safe as long as the alcohol supply lasted for them.

Because of my father's drinking problem, Mother had indoctrinated us about the evils of alcohol, so that until I went to college, I never even had a little sip of wine. At home, I was afraid to defy her. But with Mother far away in Ohio, I felt free to experiment with my life, my way.

I got putridly sick the first time I spent an evening of drinking, so sick that I felt as though I was on a rocking boat set out to sea, hit by a tidal wave, swallowed up by Moby Dick, dizzily swimming in the beast's stomach. I couldn't function for three whole miserable days and missed an important History I exam. After that experience, I really didn't care how 'goody-two-shoes' I would be to everyone else on fraternity row; drinking was not for me.

Now, alcohol-free, here I was again, flat on my back, sick at both ends and feeling like I was going to die. The girl in the next bed, more delirious than I, who had cried and moaned 24 hours a day since they brought her in, kept mumbling something about dying in her room, then she rolled over, facing me, and let loose her entire pungent innards on the floor between our beds. I half wished that she would die and let me lie there alone in quiet misery.

Some days, within the fog of my high fever, the thought crossed my mind that if I escaped being carried out of the infirmary with a white sheet over my head, that maybe I should go home to the safety of Pennsylvania Avenue, my mother's loving care, the comfort of my dog and the familiar streets of Steubenville; proof that I was indeed, at times, a wee bit delirious or, more exactly, not yet as independent as I would liked to have thought.

Finally, when I was well enough to be released from the infirmary, I never thought about going home again, at least not for a long while.

I remember hearing that the Russians launched a satellite, Sputnik, while I was dining on 'mystery meat' in the dining hall. The concept that an object like that, or anything whatsoever, could circle the earth at great speeds without blowing up, or that food as disgusting as 'mystery meat' could have been invented, was so overwhelming to all of us. Little did we know the food dilemma, as related within time frames, would pass in an eyelash as compared to what a lasting impact Sputnik would have on our future and the Space Age we were entering. Unfortunately, at the time, our biggest challenge on campus was figuring out what kind of animal we were eating when the menu rotated around to this strange tasting foodstuff.

Other than trying to guess what we were going to eat each day, there were few intellectual light bulbs that went off in our heads, and looking back, I still didn't have a clue what was going on within me, or my head. In retrospect, it seems rather farcical to assign equal concern to cafeteria food with such a great step for the human race.

In my freshman year, I pledged Delta, Delta, Delta sorority and as a sophomore moved into the sorority house at the bottom of College Hill. Institutional dormitory living had been hard for me, and after of a year of living that way, I longed to be back in a home environment. In the sorority house there was a large living room with a kitchen we could raid in the middle of the night when an attack of munchies hit and we had a grandmotherly housemother. More or less, it was as close to home as I could get.

Judy, one of my older sorority sisters, started dating a cadet at West Point whose name was Pete Dawkins. On occasion, she would invite one of the sisters up to meet with some of the other cadets that needed a date. One weekend Judy asked me to join her for a date with Pete's roommate and I was thrilled. I had heard so much about West Point and Pete's handsome roommate. I had to pinch myself to insure that I wasn't dreaming.

But the cloud of mishaps and missed opportunities that I seemed to have been dodging most of my life, thus far, followed me to West Point. My date was on curfew for low grades in several classes that weekend. He was on the football team with Pete and had to cram some studies. I spent most of my time during the day at West Point wandering around campus by myself. We double dated with Pete and Judy that night. I really liked Lee and we had a great time. He was everything Judy said he was, handsome and funny and a great dancer.

Then came Sunday. I got lost on my way to the famous West Point Chapel to meet Lee the next morning, and by the time I had found my way, I had missed him, the services had started, and the only seat left in the chapel was behind the largest architectural pillar I had ever seen in my life. The chapel pews were crowded and there wasn't any sliding leeway so that I could at least see the service. I spent the entire worship hour staring at the massive gray pillar two feet from my nose and wondering why God hadn't programmed me with better radar. Lee looked quite annoyed when we finally found each other. At that point I knew I was a dead soldier. Big men on campus are not used to waiting

Another sorority sister went up several weeks later for a date with Lee and was endowed with a better internal road map. She took the right path to the chapel and eventually wound up walking down the center aisle at West Point as his wife. So did Judy with Pete.

Somehow at Maryland after that I carefully managed to remain on the shallow edge, retaining a lack of total commitment or enthusiasm for most things: friendships, boyfriends and even my studies. I had waited for years to leave home, yet being in college did not drastically change my direction in life nor fulfill the constant emptiness tugging at me.

I am today, still at a loss to try to analyze what those years at Maryland meant to me. Looking back, there is no heavy nostalgia to get me all fuzzy when I think of my college days. Just memories of walking from the sorority house to class, up and down the steep hill, over and over and over again, and along the path past the white-pillared chapel to the red brick academic buildings.

There were no milestones I can speak of, no elevation of my social consciousness I can brag about, few memorable moments stored away. I did get to meet Louis

Armstrong, who played at our homecoming dance and Queen Elizabeth and Prince Philip who came to visit campus once, but I am embarrassed to admit the truth; that I did not develop intellectually or emotionally to any great extent. I failed to make the most of what could have been a turning point in my life. It was a wash and I was still trying to find my way.

Worst of all, I wasted money on an education I didn't appreciate; money my parents could have used to better their lives. In the end, I couldn't take it anymore and when the following semester ended, I left without any farewells. At my parents' suggestion, I went to New York and enrolled in the Katherine Gibbs School on Park Avenue and stayed at the Barbizon Hotel for Women, in a room no bigger than a closet, until I graduated. If this passage in my life seems very brief, in my mind it is. I wanted to leave Maryland and go to New York to study theater and this is the only way my parents would even consider supporting me financially. Daddy didn't want any daughter of his to be on the stage.

His stubborn conviction on the matter years earlier cautioned me to have to deal with him very carefully, so that I could eventually get my way. My cousin who lived next door to us on Pennsylvania Avenue, Carolyn, who was about ten years older than I, left Steubenville after she graduated from high school. After being under contract to Harry Conover when she arrived in New York, she soon landed a modeling contract with Eileen and Jerry Ford of the world-famous Ford Modeling Agency. While staying at the Barbizon Hotel for Women, she befriended a struggling young actress from Philadelphia, Grace Kelly, who also was staying there. As their friendship grew, so did their respective careers.

Back home, we all would buy the magazines Carolyn was in and watched the commercials and live television shows in which her friend Grace had a part. And I would dream that someday I also could go to New York and be in the theater. So, in high school, I wrote to Carolyn and asked her what I should do and she sent me this response:

Dear Sandra,

Thank you for your nice letter. I'm pleased you could wear the Capezios that I sent home. I wasn't too sure who could wear them when I sent the box of things home to Mother because I've lost track of how grown up all of you are. I should have remembered from last summer how tall you have gotten!

As far as your coming to New York to study acting, I have spoken to Grace and she is willing to sponsor you at the school she went to here, The American Academy of Dramatic Arts. She said she will contact the school and you probably will not have to audition until you arrive. With your talent and her endorsement, she thinks you might even be able to get a scholarship during your study.

I have contacted the school to send you a catalogue for you to look at. Good luck and it will be nice to have you here with us. Give my love to your parents and say hello to everyone for me.

Love, Caroline

One would have thought that with Ms. Kelly's offer to provide me a strong stepping-stone from which to build a future that I so wanted, my parents would have been pleased. But when I shared this wonderful opportunity with my father, he refused to let me go to New York. His reasoning was that I would starve to death as an actor, the stage life was not for his daughter and if I didn't go to college first, he couldn't help me.

Trying to analyze my attitude at Maryland, and later at Katherine Gibbs, I can see that my state of mind was a direct result of my father's strict control over me and my inability to get out from under it. Unfortunately, as I had hoped, removing myself physically from 1414 Pennsylvania Avenue did not lessen his hold over me until I left school and eventually attained financial freedom. However meager it was, the way I looked at it, any income I could independently generate was worth more than all the gold in Fort Knox. I finally had to start working hard to please myself, instead of my father.

When I went to Katharine Gibbs it was *the* place to send your daughters after college to give their careers a bit of polishing. Some of the students came over the bridges and through the New York tunnels to get to class, but it was the students who lived at the Barbizon that opened my eyes to a culture I only had read about in *Town & Country* Magazine. Patricia White of the White Sewing Machine and Trucking fortune lived down the hall and was constantly going to the theater with the likes of Roddy McDowell. Her father raised polo ponies in England and her mother and stepfather had a country home in Virginia. My next door neighbor was Nancy DuPont, and a few rooms down from her was Alice Blair, whose family lived on Rodeo Drive in Beverly Hills. Her brother Jim was at Princeton and Alice was always taking weekends away from the Barbizon to ride the train to Princeton Junction. Alice, eventually became my best friend at Gibbs. And then there was Lynne.

Lynne was an only child. Her father was Lew Wasserman. *The* Lew Wasserman, who at the time I knew Lynne, was the head of MCA, the star-studded talent agency, and also the head of MCA Television. Her father was one of the most powerful men in Hollywood, if not *the* most. I remember on her birthday, cards from celebrities would be covering the top of her dresser. One in particular I remember was from Alfred Hitchcock with his famous signature scrawled across the middle of the card.

Sometimes I would fantasize meeting her famous father, but none of us saw either of her parents during the entire time we were at school.

The fantasies and slight envy I had of Lynne's life soon faded when I realized that she appeared to be one of the loneliest girls I had ever met. When she came to school, her parents moved, and didn't set up a room for her in their new house. At least that is what she told us. At home she often took her meals by herself because her parents were always out, dining with the Hollywood elite. They were the larger-than-life figures at the top of the pyramid. This particularly seemed odd to me since mealtimes at our house was always a time our family enjoyed being together, in spite of Mother's lack of culinary inventiveness. Of course, that was before the days of TV dinners and snack trays, but still, it was an important family time and I couldn't imagine the isolation of eating alone.

Lynne had a well-founded mistrust of friends who might want to be around her because of her powerful father. At school, she had a small group that she knew from California and my friend Alice was one of them. That is how I got to know her, through Alice, otherwise I'm quite certain I would not have been trusted to be her friend. But Lynne was strong and I knew she would survive and have a life of her own, in spite of her unusual environment.

So, I suppose I could say that my days at Katherine Gibbs did have a lasting impact upon me and I learned important life lessons while there. I was fortunate to have made what turned out to be several lasting friendships, and I also saw with my own eyes that power and money were not as glamorous as I was lead to believe in the pages of my magazines.

After graduation, Alice went back to California and Patricia White and I eventually wound up as roommates in an apartment on East 79th Street. I found a job working for a designer in the garment district on West 41st Street and Patricia took a job at the publishing house, Simon & Schuster. My weekly salary was quickly gobbled up by my share of the rent, plus acting and voice classes. But, providing for myself and doing what I enjoyed gave me new energy and focus I had not had since my campaign to leave home. In my classes I regained the confidence I had lost during my bout with rheumatic fever. Even my teachers bolstered my belief in my talent with encouragement and for the first time in years, I felt I was headed in the right direction.

To save money, I'd bag my lunch and on nice days, sit in the park behind the New York Public Library close to my office. I watched with envy as lovers, under the spell of the first throws of the 'touchy-feely' romance, kiss and whisper secret amours to each other, their open passions making the rest of us in the park totally invisible to them. I watched '9-to-5ers' in their white shirts and ties, tired of punching the same old clock, scan the newspapers for the next job; a way out of their humdrum.

Though I made sure I got a bench far away from them, I felt not only compassion, but also a certain respect for the methodic preparations by the homeless and troubled wanderers in the park. Day after day, they busied themselves by gently folding discarded newspapers, as though they were cloths of fine silk, which they often used for hats or blankets or just to fill their sacks for another day.

All of these park people I observed became players in my matinee theater and sometimes I gave them fictitious lives and stories. The skinny gray squirrels that nervously scampered about the trees; the fat pigeons, so overfed they wobbled like penguins, over here, then over there; they, along with me, were the audience for these live performances in Bryant Park.

I used to walk at the end of the day from work to home, which was a good thirty-eight uptown blocks and a another six long blocks cross town. I usually walked up Fifth Avenue past the Plaza Hotel on 59th, then cut east a little further up to Madison and at 79th, turn and walk toward the river and home.

As I made my way uptown, well-groomed women would be quickly gliding in and out of the canopied buildings on Fifth Avenue with their tanned skins, silk scarves and big sunglasses shielding them from the stares of nibby-nose nobodies like me. Those big dark sunglasses that kept the rest of us away from their exclusive world. Big dark sunglasses that kept secret what went on in the lives of the thin, tan skinned women who lived in the doormen buildings on Fifth Avenue. All the way home up Madison, passing the shop windows. The tempting displays of diamonds and designer fashions made me envious of the rich, pampered, tan and sunglassed women of Fifth Avenue.

I needed a piano. In our one bedroom apartment, we barely had furniture, let alone a piano, which I desperately needed to practice my singing. There was a piano living above us and when I found out it's owner was the gentleman with the little fuzzy dog I often saw in the elevator, I got my confidence up to barter with him. Our agreement was that I would walk his dog twice a day, once in the morning and once at night, in exchange for the use of his piano to vocalize three times a week.

The first day of our arrangement, when I entered his apartment, my jaw dropped. The walls in his living room were lined with celebrities. Larger than life pictures of Marlena Deitrich, Ethel Merman and many of the other big time celebrities I had either seen in the movies or on television. I was in awe of his weighty wall to say the least. I was so impressed with those pictures. I figured he must know each and every one of them personally, that even after about three weeks of walking his dog and vocalizing in his apartment while he was away, I would slowly circle the room looking at the pictures as though I were in a fine art gallery.

Once, by mistake, I left my practice tape on his piano and didn't miss it until he knocked on our door that same night while my roommates and I were having a party. "I hope you don't mind, but I listened to your tape. Would you be interested in coming up to my apartment to talk to me about it?"

A normal girl who believed in her talent would have jumped at the chance to discuss her career with someone who had such important pictures on his wall, unfortunately not me. Today, I still can't believe my reaction to his proposal. In my skewered mind, I thought, 'Ooh, a dirty old man who is trying to sleep with me.' And so I never went up to his apartment again, nor walked his dog, nor used his piano. In the bat of a gnat's eyelash I lost a job, a piano and perhaps the opportunity of a lifetime.

Much later I read about him in the newspaper. He was Ethel Merman's manager and unfortunately for me, an important man who thought I had talent. And I left him standing in the hallway, my door closing awkwardly in his face. How my life would have turned out had I been just a little smarter and not so afraid of myself, I'll never know.

I kept in touch with Carolyn and saw her often while I was studying and working. By the time I finally got to New York, Grace had already become a movie star and had also become royalty by marrying the handsome head of the royal family of Monaco, Prince Rainier. Carolyn was one of Grace's bridesmaids and on her return from Monaco, I remember proudly watching my cousin during a post-wedding interview with Dave Garroway on NBC's Today Show. Although it has since been written that Grace wasn't pleased that Carolyn consented to do the interview, I today question that supposition. But if it is true, Grace had gotten over it by the time I met her. At that time the world could not get enough information about our Princess Grace and her fairy tale romance. Including me. And as luck would have it, I finally got to meet Princess Grace, the celebrated actress who had been willing to mentor my career.

I had been invited to spend the weekend at my cousin's spacious house that she and her husband built on Sherman Fairchild's estate, overlooking Oyster Bay in Long Island. Grace was coming for lunch on Saturday. I remember I was very nervous, but the anticipated day was one that I will cherish forever. The Princess Grace I met was far from the reserved, stiff woman I would read about later after her tragic death. To me she was warm and funny and quite down-to-earth.

During her visit with Carolyn, she did our horoscopes and we laughed at ourselves for being so serious about our star signs. She predicted that I would be very successful and that later in life I would find my greatest success and greatest love.

I speak very rarely about my one meeting with Grace because, after all, it was just a passing blip in the scheme of things. But she was warm and beautiful and I will always remember the image of her curled up on the couch, her feet free from her fine leather shoes she'd dropped to the floor. A good friend of my cousin's who had dropped by for the day, eager to catch up quickly where she had left off. As I look on it now, Grace seemed to be a good friend securing the bonds between her and Carolyn that were threatened by a time and a world away.

A steady diet of Dannon yogurt from the corner A&P and cheesecake at the Horn & Hardart automat where I would put 25 cents into the slot to release the cake from its little cubicle and an occasional knish from the delicatessen became my primary food sources. Although the price was right, and they gave me lots of energy producing carbohydrates, these foods alone were not exactly the well-balanced diet to keep my body in tip-top shape. Working long hours to pay for my studies and not eating a well-balanced diet finally took a toll on my immune system. For several months, I dragged myself about the city feeling that if I could just get more sleep I would be okay. But somehow, what sleep I did get, never seemed to make me feel better. Patricia forced me to visit her doctor and after a blood test, I was told that I had mononucleosis.

So finally, after two years of studying and struggling in New York, I reluctantly went back to Steubenville to recover over Thanksgiving and then again at Christmas, and during that time at home, I fell in love in the town I so wanted to put behind me. Thus, that was the end of my New York story. At least for awhile.

6

I met the man who I knew was the love of my life back home in Steubenville. His name was Bill. On weekends we would squeeze our naked canvas boards, paint pigments and our tall bodies into his sky-blue Volkswagen beetle and travel to the bucolic countryside on the edges of his hometown of Pittsburgh. Sometimes we would climb high above the city on the incline car that ran on tracks up the steep cliff to Mt. Washington. There we would spend lazy afternoons dressing our canvases with a collage of acrylic urban colors of the panoramic metropolitan views, including the point the three rivers, Monongahela, Allegheny, and Ohio meet at the Golden Triangle below.

At sunset, from our eagle's nest, the dying rays of the sun would set one last fire and the Steel City would be turned into a spectacular show; a gilded mirage of buildings with sparkling windows of gold. Then as the sun breathed it's last quiet sigh of the day, the city was extinguished by darkness, leaving only the twinkling embers of the faint lights below. Bill and I would hold hands, lovers held in a moment in time by the silent beauty of that golden display.

We were married in a small family ceremony one sunny morning in April and we left for Florida and our honeymoon that afternoon. I had saved myself for marriage, waited for the right man to come along in my life, so that I had no idea until after we were on our honeymoon that most of the time, he couldn't perform. How ironic for me, to have remained a virgin all those years, only to fall in love with someone who was sexually dysfunctional.

Unfortunately for both of us, we were married in a time just before the studies of Masters and Johnson and open forums about sex and male/female relationships were available. For us, in the early sixties, sexual problems were a very private matter. We were living at the tail end of the dark ages of sexual awareness and there were territories we dared not explore or expose. One of them was male impotence. Unfortunately, I couldn't pick up a magazine or turn on daytime television like I could today to help me realize that our problem was not unique.

It's not that our union was a total disaster and the final truth is we genuinely loved each other and to this day we are the best of friends. The good from our relationship is that on two of those very rare occasions of intimacy, we conceived two beautiful daughters, Brett and Alison. I will be forever grateful to him for that, but back then our continuing intimacy problems left a big, black hole in our marriage that would not heal.

Recently, Bill confided to me that he needs mystery in a relationship. Familiarity kills his concept of romance and those elements he needs to sustain a relationship. I, on the other hand, need the comfort of knowing; sharing thoughts, moments, familiar things. Looking forward to growing old together and becoming one is comforting to me. I am not afraid of complete intimacy. I long for it. It gives me great comfort to think I will walk hand in hand with someone I love into the sunset. After nearly forty years of brief multiple marriages and relationships, Bill is still at square one. I remember him telling me before we parted that he couldn't seek counseling, because if he found there was nothing to help him, he might as well jump off a bridge. It was because of his narrow reasoning that I couldn't go on with our marriage the way it was. I was not willing to jump with him.

Bill and I were emotional volcanoes of hurt, carrying with us an emptiness that overshadowed all the other good aspects of our relationship. He felt that he didn't deserve my love and slowly started pushing me away. It was as though my words of love for him made him look over his shoulder to see if I was speaking to .someone else. The empty feeling of failure, exacerbated by the sense of not being able to do anything about it, the utter weakness of that, propelled his need to turn away and turn further inward for defense. Not against me or who I was, but because of his cumulative failures as a sexual partner.

I took his insecurity as rejection and felt isolated. What common bonds that did hold our platonic marriage together were slowly being unconsciously untied by him, one by one. He wanted to free me because he loved me. I felt that life had played a dirty trick on me. I loved Bill as the friend he had become to me, as the father of my daughters, but I yearned to experience life as I had dreamed it would be with normal sexual intimacies that bond husband and wife.

After six years of living as friends, not lovers, our marriage finally fell apart and we got divorced. Bill was resigned and moved to San Francisco to build a new life. I couldn't understand how Bill could remove himself by going so far way from his daughters and I tried to convince him otherwise. But he was determined to fly away in search of outside challenges that would help him forget his inward hurts. I was resigned, too, but with a new sense of discovery of my inner-self.

Right after Bill and I were married, my parents had bought an old historic house about 18 miles west of

Steubenville, in a small town called Hopedale. Hopedale was located in the beautiful Ohio countryside, far enough away from the mills and pollution and this move was an answer to my mother's prayers. She, too, finally got away from Steubenville to a house that they owned and back into the sunshine she had rarely seen since we left Grandpa's farm. She was now where she belonged; in a palace of her own; a place she could finally call home.

My parents' new house was a big old Victorian with twelve rooms and high ceilings. The front porch wrapped around the house and was filled with white wicker sofas and chairs my mother salvaged from the barn and slicked up with coats and coats of white paint. The old house itself had been a part of John Brown's Underground Railroad during the Civil War.

Caves had been carved out of the dirt basement during that period to hide run away slaves coming through to points north and, hopefully, to safety. Resting like battered old soldiers at attention along the sagging shelves were the many wooden boxes of empty medicine bottles used to treat the slaves that sought haven in the basement hiding places. Several small cots, rusting away quietly, hand-woven cloth now hanging loosely from the frames, rotting from age and dampness, were still where they were placed a century ago, against the far opening of one of the caves. Busy spiders had taken up residence spinning webs between the feeble legs of the beds, indicating that a level of undisturbed life was still going on down there.

My parents somehow did not feel the need to remove any of this from its hiding place. My father was born south of the Mason-Dixon and was cared for by a free-woman named Minerva. She, along with her daughter, Rosy, were considered family and my father never lost his love for his old "Mammy", even after she and Rosy died. I always reasoned that my father, by keeping the cellar intact, the way it had been during the times Minerva's people were fleeing for their lives, he was, in his simple way, honoring her memory and her people and their struggle to be free.

Hopedale was also the home of a young Clark Gable, the famous movie star. As a young boy, he would visit the children who lived in my parent's house and there was a picture verifying that fact in the Clark Gable Museum; a small white salt box building on Highway 22 nearby. Hanging on the wall in that museum is a picture of Clark as a young teen sitting on the railing of our big porch.

The children and I arrived in Hopedale for the Christmas holidays with a great mixture of sadness and excitement. This would be our first Christmas without Bill. I knew my children were having a difficult time coping with the divorce and the added sorrow of their father moving so far away from them. Since they always looked forward to spending time at Grandma and Grandpa's new house, this was the best present I could give them.

In the summer, Daddy would give them a basket of apples and bits of carrots from the garden to carry up to feed the horses that grazed behind the wooden fence beyond the grassy knoll at the back the house. They would bravely drag the basket that was almost as big as they were up to the weathered fence. I can still see Alison's and Brett's tiny fingers held delicately forward, balancing each treat on the flat of their hands. It was an invitation for the horses to nuzzle their soft lips and chin hairs that tickled their eager palms while tasting their wares.

7

"Pop goes the weasel and the Jack-In-The Box jumps out of his house and that means it's time for the Romper Room School and this is Miss Sandra saying hello to all the boys and girls here and to all our friends at home."[1]

Desperate for work and money after my divorce, Mother talked me into going to an audition for the syndicated children's program, created and owned by Bert Claster in Baltimore, Maryland. The show was called *Romper Room.*

I remembered a conversation I had had with Shari Lewis, the creator of the children's show starring her hand puppet, Lambchop, several months prior to my divorce from Bill. We were both performing (I was singing) at a March of Dimes telethon in Pittsburgh and during our time off camera, we talked about her work with children and how fulfilling it was for her. Since I also enjoyed children, I thought it was something, I could do. I never thought the opportunity to try would soon fall into my lap.

Six months after my conversation with Sherri, I was auditioning for *Romper Room*. Each of the hopefuls at the audition was called into the television studio one by one for an interview with the program syndication's representatives. From that, a final cut was made to decide which of us actually would get to audition. From those finalists the winner would be hired to host the show.

Although I was nervous, my interview must have gone well, as I made the final cut. When my turn came to enter the studio, I was asked to make up a show, to pull it right from the top of my head on the spot. This performance was to include singing, talking to imaginary children, and doing several commercials. I thought of my lunches in Bryant Park and the imaginary plays I would perform in my head while watching the characters there. I knew I could sing, especially since I had sung and played Peter, Paul and Mary's "Puff the Magic Dragon" at least a thousand times for my own children on the guitar.

But, the confidence boost I got from my initial interview and my capabilities in the other areas quickly sank to zero when they asked me to saddle up on a bright orange pogo stick, a little thing made for four-years olds. In high heels and a tight mini skirt I galloped around the studio like an idiot. How I could have ever considered making a fool of myself like this and why on earth I could have let my mother convince me that I would be perfect for this job, I'll never know.

"I always knew you could do it," she said. Thanks to my mother's unending faith in her daughter, my first job after my divorce from Bill was on *Romper Room* and this stroke of good fortune changed my life forever.

Before I was allowed to go on the air, the Claster family put me into their training class in Baltimore with their daughter, Sally, who had taken over for her mother, Nancy, as my teacher. Miss Nancy had been the original Romper Room teacher and when Nancy retired, Miss Sally inherited her mother's position. Sally, a stylishly slender young woman with short dark hair, was an excellent teacher and put me through the paces of a real live show during the week I was in training.

One session was held in the Claster home, and at one point, I was comfortably seated on the living room couch that had the most interesting black and white tweed fabric. Trying to score some brownie points, I let her know how much I loved the 'tweed fabric'. Her face showed a slight wonderment at my remark. And it wasn't until later when their two lively Dalmatian dogs bounded into the room to jump into our laps, that I realized that the solid black upholstered couch was filled with needle sharp hairs from the dogs that had creatively woven themselves into the fabric of their lovely couch. From that time on, I carefully kept my opinions to myself.

Although I went into my first live telecast feeling fully ready, nothing in my wildest dreams prepared me for the moment when the floor assistant began the countdown to airtime. I began to hyperventilate and I thought how stupid I was for wearing a bow blouse, because the bow, having been activated in an interesting jump, jump-a-de-jump, jump-a-de-jump movement by my racing heart, was bouncing spastically against my cheek. My legs felt like rubber and never regained consciousness as I woodenly went through my paces on the set. If there had been a man with a big hook on the side, like I had seen in The Three Stooges comedies, I would have been ever so grateful to have been pulled off, so I could run away. No such luck!

After the show was finally over, I don't know what I did to deserve such grace, but somehow, some kind of divine intervention must have been at work on my behalf. I got through the show without fainting or having my knees buckle and I didn't get fired.

As Miss Sandra, I went to the television station at eight and after a little pre-air preparation, went on the air at nine. In an hour I was finished and back at my desk, reviewing my mail. I only interviewed prospective students once a week, so on most days, by noon, I was heading back home to my children. Working half a day on a job that provided well for us was perfect and I got the needed creative stimulation I craved. My young dreams to be on the screen as an actor, through this show, realized a small corner of my ambitions. I felt fortunate that my new life was working out so well.

The Romper Room scripts arrived in my mail at the station on a weekly basis from headquarters in Baltimore. I was warned ahead of time by Miss Sally that I was not allowed to deviate one inch from the script unless it said so. I had to follow to the letter the program script, week by week, or risk getting fired. As an example, I was told that one Romper Room teacher took it upon herself to include the children's song..."Itsy, bitsy spider climbing up the spout," an often sung ditty most little children know. Well, her decision to divert from the original script made "Itsy, bitsy spider climbing up the spout," not only her downfall, but also her swan song on Romper Room. She was fired for not sticking to the script. So, on those many occasions when the scripts repeated themselves and I was tempted to add some of my own creativity beyond the natural interplay with my students, I had to hold back in fear of being terminated.

The Romper Room years were good ones for me in several ways. First, I loved getting up and going to work. I liked working with children and I enjoyed each group of Do Bees as they came, then 'graduated' after two weeks to make room for the next class. Secondly, the hours and hours of live television experience was a perfect training ground which would eventually enable me move on to something else in television after I tired of Romper Room. Because year after year the scripts often repeated themselves, I knew I would eventually crave more of a challenge at work. What or when that next step for me would be, I wasn't sure, but I was preparing.

My office at the station was next to the news department and sometimes, after my administrative work was done, I would pop my head into the newsroom now and then to read the AP wire or make small talk with the writers and anchormen. I know they were pleased when I dropped by to have some diversion from the angst of the stories that make news headlines when I dropped by, but I also knew, because I was a woman and they enjoyed flirting with me, that none of them took me seriously. I was fluff that, at best, might work out as a weather girl, if I ever tired of Romper Room. How hard could it be to read the wires or call up the National Weather Bureau for current information on local weather? Even a woman could do that, was their unified and unspoken attitude toward anyone of my gender.

8

I had been on Romper Room for about a year, my children and my work being the center of my life. Until, quite by chance, I met someone. It was the week before Christmas in 1968 and light snow had been dusting all day, so by evening when I left the house to meet friends at the Pittsburgh Press Club's holiday party, a glittering layer of white had already cloaked the city landscape. As I drove from the suburbs through the tunnel and out into the Golden Triangle, my tires scrunched and squeaked as they rolled through the unplowed streets to my destination.

By the time I parked my car in the municipal garage and walked a block to the party, the powdery snow covered my hair and coat shoulders. Having unfashionably naturally curly hair in a fashionably straight world was a curse, I thought, as I made an attempt to brush the wetness from my hair with my gloves. I had taken such pains, preparing for this rare evening out, rolling my hair in curlers the size of frozen orange juice cans to force my unwilling locks to go against their nature. It all had been for nothing.

"Now don't waste your time trying to make a silk purse out of a sow's ear, young lady. Your curly locks you got from me, and they've suited me just fine,"

Grandma used to say as she pulled and tugged at my golden mass of kink, taming the wildness on top of my head into thick braids tied with rubber bands at the ends. Much better her fussing with my hair than my mother, who would make the plats so tight my scalp would hurt for days. 'Well, Grandma,' I said underneath my curly head that I could almost hear squeaking as it dried, getting higher and wider by the time I handed my coat to the attendant, 'This is not 1895, it is now, and curly hair sucks!'

I avoided all mirrors on the way to the ballroom to escape the Frankenstein's Bride-hairdo suspended above my Betty Davis eyes and new black sheath cocktail dress image. I joined my friends at their table and they discreetly avoided staring at my mile high head. "What a lovely dress, it's great for your figure." And I thought, aren't good friends grand; unconditional acceptance, just like my dog BJ, who loved me, just because I am?

I ordered a Coke, tried to forget about my hair, and made an effort to focus on the animated conversation at our table. Suddenly, my attention was diverted and my eyes caught a figure moving toward our table. As he came nearer and moved into the light, the same feeling of passion came over me that I had had when I first watched Ingrid Bergman and Humphry Bogart in their famous love scene in 'Casa Blanca.'

In my voluminous head, violins began playing and fog rose about his feet as he glided our way. Before me stood the most handsome man I had ever seen in my life; tall with dark wavy hair that was thick and spilled curls softly across his forehead. His ruddy complexion wore a slight hint of a five o'clock shadow and his cheekbones were high and strong as though constructed to contain the inferno within his green eyes. Aware that I was gaping at him, our eyes connected and I felt a warm tingling inside. I and my mile- high-hairdo were in love. I had to have this man.

The same grandma that shamed me for hating my curly hair, also imparted other words of wisdom that made me want to stick my fingers in my ears, ears that were always exposed, I might add, due to the braids she was so pleased with. Grandma would tell me when I was out of sorts that "out of bad things always comes something good, if you're smart enough to look for it." I never believed her, until now.

In spite of my 'bad hair' day, Jennings asked me for a date after New Year's Eve, then another and another and then, asked me to share his life forever. I couldn't believe that I just happened into this man. This man who walked into my life; a man who women forever would watch with lust in their eyes as he walked though a room. This man wanted to walk with me 'till death do us part.' And with my acceptance of that choice, in the end, I got the treasured surprise at the bottom of the Cracker Jack box.

My philosophy about life is that it comprises constant choices. And the ebbs and flows in our lives, the highs and lows, by all accounts are controlled by those choices. As my father so often reminded me, I wore my heart on my sleeve and in hindsight, most of my choices in my life have had emotional, not logical roots. And perhaps it is a weakness I'll carry to my grave, if it can be qualified as a weakness, because I'm not too sure I've gotten it right yet, if there is such thing as a 'right.'

I had always planned to be one of those grownup people who made the right decisions; went to the right schools; got the right grades; married the right man; had the right amount of healthy, brilliant children; said the right things; had the right friends and inherited the right to always be right. And I may be right when I wonder if it's too late to happen to me, to late to finally get it right.

When I posed this question to myself before I married Jennings, I replied to myself with great hope for our future together, "As long as we're still breathing and choosing, there's hope for all of us to get it right sometime in our lives."

Another bride, another bridegroom, another beginning for me. I had married my prince and the emotionally empty life I had turned into a fairy tale. Jennings and I were married in a private ceremony with his sister and brother-in-law standing as witnesses for us. It didn't matter to me what kind of service we had. All I knew was that I was madly in love and wanted to spend the rest of my life with Jennings. I wanted to share his pajamas, his days; have his children and grow old with him. I felt I was one of the few who had so many things to be thankful for in my life. I had two beautiful children, the love of a wonderful new husband, and of course, my work on Romper Room.

Even though I was the teacher on Romper Room, in a way, I grew up, too, while doing the show. I never experienced the depth of my feelings for children until I first became a mother; then Miss Sandra on the show. It is from those years working with the children on Romper Room that I began to realize the purity and strength of a child's unconditional love and what a special gift that is. Each student that walked on the set became special to me and I valued each of their letters and pictures; primary-colored works truly created in an effort to express love for their teacher.

Brett and Alison always came to personal appearances with me, but they were very curious as to what the fuss was all about. After all, I was only the woman who made their peanut butter sandwiches in my pajamas; made them wash behind their ears and walked around the house in hair curlers. I was just a mother, so what was the big deal? But, they were always happy to fill an extra seat if one of my little Do Bee's were sick and had to miss a show. The only requirement, other than not eating too many chocolate Hostess cupcakes, was to please try to remember to call me 'Miss Sandra' instead of 'Mommy', while playing with their Romper Room friends.

So, because I enjoyed being a mother and I loved my new husband I was ready to get pregnant someday, but not too soon. In spite of the ever-present reality that my biological clock was ticking away, my life was full and I wanted to savor everything I had right now. I wasn't quite ready to have another baby yet. But my husband wanted a child and I was soon to discover my thoughts on the subject meant nothing to him. Jennings had other plans for his wife.

9

My marriage to Jennings opened up a whole world of sexuality and fulfillment that I never knew existed. I loved when he moved next to me, pressing his body against the small of my back, the warmth of him. Even the smell of him was intoxicating and wonderful. It was so late in life that I knew the joys of intimacy and my husband had always been the gentlest of teachers. I trusted him with my body and had no signs or reasons to expect anything other. Until one night when I knew it would be a perfect time in my cycle for conceiving, and I turned away from him.

I tried to put him off by telling him I wasn't in the mood because I had had a tiring day, so I kissed him and rolled over to turn out the light. I startled when he gripped my shoulder and pulled me around. When I looked at him I could see rage beyond anything I had ever witnessed. His eyes were blazing.

Before I could react with some movement in defense of his aggression, he pressed his body on mine and held my hands above my head in a grip so tight I could feel my hands pulsing and my fingers going numb. He became an animal and pulled and pushed inside me. I was too frightened to move after he had satisfied himself.

From somewhere deep within, I did cry out, a silent, involuntary primal scream that roared through my brain, but there was no one there to hear me; to protect me; to care. I was his wife. After he had ravaged me, he gave me a gloating smack on my hind cheek, turned his back to me and I silently cried myself to sleep.

The next morning I stayed in bed and pretended to be asleep until Jennings left the house for work. My body ached and resisted my efforts to leave the bed. I walked over to the mirror and pulled down the edge of my nightgown, exposing my shoulder. My image revealed an ugly purple bruise on my right shoulder where he pulled me around and slammed me against the bed. I moved closer to the mirror and could see my face was raw where his beard had dug into my skin, using my face like a wild animal scratching his back on a tree.

My gown was torn to my waist and I saw what I expected; numerous bruises between my legs and down my calves where his hands had groped me. I couldn't raise my arms because of the excruciating pain when I tried to slip my nightgown over my head, so I removed it by sliding it off my shoulders and dropping it on the floor around my feet.

My eyes returned to the mirror and I stood there naked, chilled by the morning cold of the room, and confronted the mirrored image of me. Looking at my battered body, I could not deny what Jennings had done. I had been raped and at that moment last night, all of the trust and passion for the husband I had cherished had been erased.

I walked into the bathroom and took two aspirin from the medicine cabinet and washed down the gritty tablets with cold water from the tap. I stepped into the shower and turned the faucet head to allow the warm water caress my swollen body parts. I wondered if there was enough makeup to cover my facial burns and counted on my violated body not to fail me on the show. But the wounds inside my mind could not be covered up so magically and I mourned for a loss that was so overwhelming I couldn't even begin to confront it.

Unaware of the thought processes so many emotionally abused women execute, especially those children of alcoholics, I took the blame. After all, I reasoned, everybody loves Jennings. From the moment they met him, my friends all thought he was terrific. He was highly respected at the alloy business he owned. He was an inventor. He was smart. He was handsome. He was everything a woman could ask for. How could they all be so wrong in their appraisal of him?

The more hours and then days that passed, and the more I thought about that night and played over again the painful events in my mind, the more I began to convince myself that maybe it was my fault. Because I refused my husband the one great thing we had together, I bore the responsibility. Maybe there was a chance that I unwittingly caused the entire incident. In the end, I convinced myself that what happened that night was probably my fault. And I shoved it under the rug with the rest of my emotional dirt.

Jennings got what he wanted. From that painful night, I became pregnant. After having gone through two pregnancies, I knew I was not one of the lucky ones who could breeze through the first trimester without morning sickness. And, sure enough, for the next three months I went to work very green, hoping I wouldn't throw up on the set.

The once tempting aroma of the endless snacks made me nauseous five days a week for the entire ninety-day period and then my nausea turned into a craving for grapefruits. I would devour them, with juice dripping from my chin. I had an insatiable desire for citrus and was sending anyone I could grab going out of the station to bring me back a fresh supply. It got so that the entire news staff would come to the station in the morning armed with bags of the fruit, just to keep me from annoying them.

They were all convinced that I was a citrus junkie and that my child would definitely be born with a Vitamin C high.

We had been living in the house Bill and I had bought when suddenly, out of the blue, Jennings decided that since a new baby was coming, we should look for a new place, a home of our own. I wasn't too thrilled with the idea. Like my mother, I needed a nest of my own and I had put down roots. How could he ask me to give all of that up? But, relentless in his goal, and day by day he pounded away at me with his need to move into a home that didn't have Bill's memories around. Finally, worn down and taking the course of least resistance, my past repeated itself. As I always had done with my parents, I caved in to him. I gave him his way.

It was an emotionally trying day for me when I cut the last remaining cord to my life with Bill and our shared memories in that house. As the last piece of furniture was loaded on the van, I turned to take one final look at the brick house with the big double doors standing empty and so forlorn on the hill. I saw the tree in the front yard that Bill and I had planted when our first child was born; the bare branches now exposed, undressed by the cold winds of November, reaching out to me as if to caution me. Silently begging me not to leave it standing guard, the lone sentinel of my memories.

A chill touched me and I wrapped my coat around my expanded body as I climbed into the van. As we pulled away from the house, I turned and stared at the road ahead, trying not to think about what was happening. As soon as my pregnancy progresses, when I start feeling better again, I told myself, everything would be the same as it was and my life would fall neatly back into place. Our lives will regain some normalcy in our new house. Oh, I wanted it to be right. I wanted it to be right for our new child, for all of us. I had to make it work. I knew this seed of Jenning's that I carried inside of me would securely bond us again and we would share the joys of this new life that was part of each of us. I tried to convince myself everything would be okay.

It wasn't consciously clear to me at the time, but I was once again losing control of my life and a slow calculated isolation from all that was familiar to me was beginning.

Our new house in Washington, Pennsylvania, Jennings' hometown, was closer to the television station, providing I took the winding back roads across the countryside. A shorter drive also meant that I could be home more quickly at the end of my day. Home to the children. Looking back, that is the only positive thing I can remember about our move from Hankey Farms.

By mid-December, my morning sickness was slowly beginning to disappear and I was almost feeling human again. The children eagerly awaited my return from work each day so that we could continue getting the house ready for Christmas.

Bill and I would go all out when we were together and crazily buy the biggest tree we could find that would often scrape our living room cathedral ceiling. The darn thing would have to be decorated on the floor before we could hoist it upright so that the rest of the ornaments could be hung by standing on the small ladder.

Things would be different this year. Jennings was busy with his work, so this Christmas it would be just the girls and I doing the decorating. I dug through some of the unpacked boxes and found old ornaments that had long ago lost their tops and no longer would be hung on the tree. They would serve holiday duty by filling glass bowls, tucked among pine branches and tiny wooden sleighs. I even saved a few small ones to ride around and around in the open cars on the train circling the tree.

I decided to put the tree up the morning of Christmas Eve, so Jennings secured it in the holder. I reminded him that Mother and Daddy would be at the house by late afternoon and that dinner would be at seven. The girls quickly got to work placing the ornaments on the tree and I disappeared into the kitchen to perform my magic with the turkey.

By five o'clock that afternoon the tree was decorated and the aroma of roast turkey and chestnut dressing filled the house. The girls bathed and dressed in their best outfits. We were all in holiday mood and I couldn't wait for Jennings to come home so I could surprise him under the mistletoe in the hallway.

Mother and Daddy arrived about an hour later, loaded down with packages and the children excitedly helped carry their bags up to the guestroom. I still hadn't been able to unpack everything, but we cleverly covered the boxes with sheets and placed pine boughs over them with sprigs of fresh holly from a tree in the back yard.

Even though my parents had little money during some of those early years in Ohio, Santa always managed to provide my brother and me with a good Christmas. I vowed to carry on the warm memories I had of Christmas' past with my own children, no matter what.

Dinner was ready by seven. The table looked like it came straight out of the Ladies Home Journal Christmas issue and the turkey was done to a succulent golden brown. The clock in the living room chimed seven times. Jennings was late. I called his office. There was no answer. He should be on his way, I thought. I knew my parents were starving after their long drive, so by eight o'clock, the food was getting cold. I started serving dinner.

We all gathered around the beautiful table that night and dined without my husband. The table cleared; dishes done; the evening ended. Jennings never surfaced. Late that night he called and said he had an emergency at the plant and would be home late. He promised to be home in time for the children to open their packages. I didn't believe his story, but I couldn't start something with him over the phone in front of my parents. Jennings never did come home that night.

Christmas morning came and went. So did my parents. Jennings came home sometime after the children had gone to bed. He smelled of alcohol and I flew into a rage. The nerve of him! What kind of man doesn't show up for 24 hours, neglects his family during one of the most important holidays of the year, embarrasses his wife by not showing up for dinner with her parents; then comes home still half-loaded from the night before? I screamed and cried and tried to tell myself that I didn't care anymore, but I did. I was angry, hurt and afraid. I felt a knot twisting in the pit of my stomach. My world was falling apart.

Jennings spent the afternoon watching football on television. Mother called to see if everything was okay and I spent the day wondering how our marriage could have gone so wrong. I didn't understand why or how to fix it.

The days leading up to the New Year went by uneventfully, Jennings and I hardly spoke to one another, but I tried to forget, or at least rise above my anger about Christmas. I didn't even dare to ask about New Year's. His partner, Dominic, had a restaurant and we usually had dinner there and sometimes Jennings would help out by tending bar.

"Dominic needs help at the restaurant again this year. We'll have dinner and then you can take the children home. We'll celebrate then," my husband informed me that morning.. "It's better for you and our little one," he added, reaching over and gently rubbing my stomach. When he wanted his way, Jennings knew all the right moves. He kissed me gently and looked at me with those eyes - those eyes. He was so smooth. The memory of Christmas past would be just another hurt to go under my rug.

We had dinner as planned and I brought the children home. Alone again. Then I thought of Jenning's sister, Joanne, and maybe she would watch the girls if I took them to her house for a sleepover. I rang her and made the arrangements so that I could join Jennings back at Dominic's.

The road from our house to Dominic's inn was dark and winding. I had been there so many times before that I probably could have driven the road with my eyes closed. But, at night, alone, I was a little nervous and took great care reading the signs in the dark so as not to get lost. When I finally saw the lights to the Alameda Inn in the distance beyond, I was relieved.

The parking lot was already crowded at ten o'clock. I pulled in and drove around to the side entrance that lead to the bar. As I walked in I could hear the band in the main room playing loudly and the cigarette smoke that filled the room clouded my view. I made my way toward the bar, starting to feel a little uncomfortable. I looked up and down behind the bar, but my husband wasn't there, just a young man I'd never seen before pouring drafts for the crowd. Maybe he's taking a break, I thought.

Now I was really beginning to feel self-conscious. I moved away from the crowded bar area and glanced into the dining room where the band was playing. The music sounded pretty good from where I was standing. The dance floor was packed with couples, elbow to elbow, dancing closely and moving with the music. A wave of loneliness swept over me as I watched the happy crowd in the smoky room. I turned to walk back into the bar and my eyes caught a couple in the far corner of the room. I turned and looked again. My body went numb. It was Jennings and another woman dancing, holding each other tightly, their bodies connecting. I wanted to run, but I couldn't make my legs move. I just stood there and watched them kiss and caress and I wanted to die.

I felt a tap on my shoulder, "Want to dance?" he said. I shook my head from side to side, "No, I'm with Jennings." I tried to fight back the sickness inside.

"His girlfriend?"

"No, his wife," I told the stranger. "When he' finished dancing with his girlfriend, tell him I've gone home."

I ran outside and the dinner I had had earlier with my husband came rumbling up from my stomach and onto the gravel in the parking lot. I leaned my head against the car door. How stupid it was that I didn't see. He forced me to have his child. How could I have been so wrong again? I hated him and all of his lies. I knew something had been going wrong for us, but I never suspected another woman. I wanted to get as far away from him as I could. The dark drive home was long and lonely.

I went into the house and packed our clothes. Jennings did not come home that night and I was relieved. I don't think I could have handled a confrontation with him. The next morning I picked up the girl's from Joanne's and without a word drove to the safety of my parents' home. Within a week I had moved completely out of the house my loving husband had chosen. I never wanted to see Jennings ever again.

During the ensuing months, in my parents' home, I waited for the birth of my third child. I continued to go to work every day pretending to the outside world that nothing had happened, trying to put my shattered heart and life together again.

10

I can recall the following events with a kaleidoscope of emotions and it has been a struggle to keep what is on the page from intruding into my present life. It has been a very difficult task re-walking my steps, disturbing the ghosts beneath my feet. The reality of carrying a child to term, alone, without a loving husband by my side was probably one of the most mentally trying times of my life.

The shame I felt finding my husband with his mistress was so painful for me. My pride wouldn't allow me to share my circumstances with my colleagues. Only my family and close friends knew I was no longer with Jennings. The choice I made to shield my circumstances from the outside world kept me in a constant state of play-acting. It was just too uncomfortable for me to share the truth with others beyond those that I loved. The childhood pattern of safeguarding the unfortunate events in my life was well entrenched.

After a short stay with my parents, I moved my little family into a small apartment of my own above Mountford's Drugstore in Houston, a small town just outside of Washington, Pennsylvania. How far I had fallen. From a beautiful spacious home in Pittsburgh, to this; all for the love of a man.

I still drove my sporty Yenko customized hugger-orange Chevrolet Camaro to Romper Room, but at the end of the day, I was hanging out laundry on the flat tar roof that I had to access by going through my bedroom window. During the morning, Romper Room helped me forget about my life for a short time, at least on the surface, and I wore a great big smile for the world to see.

At home, surrounded by the reality of my circumstances, alone and uncertain of our future, I would lock myself in the bathroom after the girls were in bed and cry into a towel to keep them from witnessing my heartache.

July 20, 1969. I stayed up late that night to watch the first moon landing. It was absolutely incredible that our space race had come so far. It seemed only yesterday that I was in the dining hall at Maryland thinking of how Sputnik was flying about our heads up there higher than anything made by man had circled before, and as an American, questioning why didn't we get there first? Now, twelve years later, the American flag was planted firmly on the big spherical mass that illuminates our planet. We actually had men bouncing about the moon in slow motion, unstrapped by gravity. What will happen to the mystique now; this event taking away from all romanticists and writers of love songs their object of inspiration? I knew I would never be able look up at a full moon smiling down upon me and wonder in the same way ever again.

The excitement of the space landing kept me from falling into a deep sleep that night and I was still tossing about in my bed as the summer sun began to peek its head over the flat roof outside my window. The light filtering through the room ended any possibility of my trying to go back to sleep. So I decided I might as well take advantage of the morning coolness to hang the freshly washed kitchen curtains outside on the clothesline while the children were sleeping.

No sooner had I hung the last curtain and crawled back through the window, that I felt a sharp contraction. I tried to relax, thinking it might be a muscle spasm from reaching while doing the curtains. But when the second and third assault from my womb hit me, I called my neighbor to watch the girls and her husband drove me to the hospital and dropped me off at the Emergency Room door. I felt like Little Orphan Annie, suitcase in hand, eyeing the door in front of me with anxiety. But I had little time to think about it. My pain quickly pushed me forward through the door and into a waiting wheelchair.

The pain was excruciating. I hadn't remembered it being so bad. Breathe. Take a deep breath, I told myself. At least I remembered something from the births of my first two children. Another sharp cramping sensation shot though my lower back and abdomen. This time it lasted longer. I pushed the button for the nurse. The pain subsided and I breathed deeply again trying to relax my body.

I looked about the large room filled with empty beds. My bed awkwardly rested horizontally against a wide pillar in the middle and obstructed my view of the left side of the room. Hearing no noise from that side, I imagined that it, too, was vacant. No wives having sex with their husbands anymore? Too many bars and TV's in Washington, I suppose!

Another contraction came with force. They were getting closer. I'll never do this again, I vowed. Just then, a crisply uniformed nurse entered the room and checked my dilation. The pain returned. My instinct was to bear down. I couldn't help it.

"Not yet, Sweetie," the nurse said, holding my hand. "The doctor's on his way."

Again the blinding pain hit.

"Hold, on. Breathe deeply."

Just when I thought I couldn't stand it anymore, I heard footsteps, clicking; echoing down the hall, coming our way. I recognized my doctor's voice. "Okay, she's ready. Push. Now… Easy… Good...Sandra...Push. Not too hard let it come by itself. Okay! Okay! It's through...nice and easy now. Great!"

I must have lost consciousness for a minute. I heard the doctor's voice calling my name, from the bottom of a deep, deep well. I heard the doctor, but I didn't hear the baby. I held my breath. Then a marvelous sound echoed and bounced off the sterile walls of the delivery room. Sharp staccato wails. The music of a new life filled the room and my heart ached with happiness that it was finally over.

"Bet you're proud of yourself, Mama. It's a healthy boy; he's got the power in his lungs of Caruso," he laughed. We're going to clean him up and weigh him in, then Nurse will let you hold him." Dr. Haddock came around to where he could see me and gently patted my arm. "Try to get some rest now. He'll be waiting for you when you wake up. The little guy has had a hard morning, too. I'm happy for you. You got that boy you wanted."

I closed my eyes. A boy! I was hoping I wasn't dreaming and it was finally over. A lump came to my throat and I fought back mixed tears of relief and joy. Everything I had been through, the choice to bring this child to term, into the world, all the past was forgotten when I heard his first tiny cry. I vowed that this child's existence would be meaningful somehow, in some way, an existence that would go beyond the joy he brought to his sisters and me.

Later, when they brought him to me, as I held this tiny red-faced bundle in my arms, wrapped like a butterfly, partially emerging from his cocoon, I loosened the blanket and let his skinny arms free. His whole wrinkly hand was no bigger than half of my index finger. I uncurled his delicate fist and marveled at how his hand was a miniature version of his father's. I wanted to hold him forever, assure him that I would take care of him and protect him from all that is evil in the world. I wanted to hold him, drinking in the beauty of his scrunched up face, this new life that God had given us. But, too quickly, the nurse appeared and my little butterfly flew way with her to the nursery. While the world was celebrating the miracle of man on the Moon, I was celebrating our miracle of life, here on Earth. It had been a remarkable day.

I left the hospital with my baby in my arms determined to start again with my three children as the center of my life. I was not going to let my circumstances defeat me. I had learned from my mistakes and was reborn along with my son. I had not heard from Jennings, but Jennings' sister said that he had come to see his son in the hospital. I named our beautiful son Emerson Lee after his great grandfather. And that was that.

The months that followed were full of new discoveries for me. I found pleasure in my growing family and my work. I continued on Romper Room, moved in with my parents and filed for divorce from Jennings. The surprise of all surprises was that complicated my life even more, is that he didn't want a divorce and fought it.

After a few months, Jennings finally called me and pleaded for forgiveness for his mistakes. He vowed that he had always loved me and was sorry for the things he had done to hurt me. But this time I wasn't buying it. He admitted that he needed help and promised to see a therapist if I would hold off on the divorce.

Good news for you, I responded. It will help you with your next relationship. None of his ploys changed the anger I felt toward him, but I knew if I didn't go along with his request to stay the divorce, I would be in for a terrible fight. I was finished with him emotionally, so what did a few more months matter now?

Jennings continued to persist in his efforts to get me back just as strongly as he did before we were married. He called me every night, wrote sympathetic letters and made the long drive from Washington to Hopedale to see our son every weekend. He was executing all the right maneuvers in his war to take my heart again. But as strong as I thought I had become, I was no match for him.

My husband had been in therapy for a year when Lee celebrated his second birthday. I had taken an anchor position, in addition my own talk show at the station. Not only would it mean more financial security for us, but it would also give me the creative direction I had always desired. I was taken up by this direction and opportunity in my career and was not about to take on the responsibility of trying to making Jennings happy, too.

11

I can remember the pivotal point in my life when I decided to return to Jennings. I had been living at my parents' for almost three years. One evening after work I was reading Dr. Seuss's popular children's book, *Green Eggs And Ham,* to Lee while he sat quietly on my lap with his big brown eyes absorbing the details of each picture as I went along. When I finished the story and closed the book, he opened the book again with his chubby little hands and then just as suddenly, turned his head upward toward me and asked, "Mommy, do I have a daddy?"

I am ashamed to admit that during the time that I had been separated from his father, I never once thought about the effect that it would have on my son. I had just assumed that what he didn't know at this point in his life, wouldn't hurt him. But with that one sentence, a shot went through my heart that opened my eyes. I knew I couldn't deprive Lee from having the chance to allow his father to know and love him, and in return, give his son the opportunity to bond with his natural father. I realized that I had to go back to Jennings and try to make our marriage work this time. I had to believe that Jennings still loved me and that he was honest in his efforts to change his life. For Lee's sake, I had to try.

My parents were in disbelief when I told them I was going to reconcile with Jennings. They thought I had lost my senses. And although I knew I was hurting them by disregarding their advice, within a month the children and I moved out of their home and into one of our own. Jennings had found a house for us and we began anew.

In the beginning, it seemed to be working out for us. I became more confident that everything would be in place as it was at that moment. Jennings also radiated a sense of security in his belief that he finally had his life back on track again. He and I started going to Sunday services at our local Presbyterian Church; he joined the community baseball team and I continued with my career. For the first time since my marriage to Jennings five years before, I started to think that maybe I wouldn't have to worry about tomorrow.

My staff at work used to kid me that my biggest fan club was behind bars. Inmates doing time have a lot of it on their hands. Television is the strongest link to the outside world when in prison and I was there to entertain them. I was always accessible to my viewers. I felt I owed it to them. After all, it was their loyalty that paid my bills. One afternoon after my talk show, a call was put through to my office.

"Hey, kid, I really love your show." The man continued in his graveled-voice "Why don't you meet me in the parking lot behind the fire house. I'm a big fan of yours. I'll show you just how big I am."

For once, I was speechless. I quickly hung up the phone in disgust. Now, if that first call had been the last, I wouldn't have thought much about it and written it off as a prank. But that call was to be just the beginning of numerous calls this man made to the station. Then as if that wasn't enough, letters started arriving in my mail. Letters declaring undying love for me; scary letters that were obviously written by a deranged person.

Appearances I had to make in conjunction with my job had to be honored, so I began going to them with either my husband or my director as bodyguards. I was always cautious about being in public alone. I made sure of my surroundings and pre-planned my travel agendas while at those events. To this point in my life, challenges became the norm, but this time, I was facing one that could affect my safety. I wished it was just a bad nightmare and that I would wake up in the morning with reality releasing me. But the reality was the truth that someone was after me and I could not shake the constant fear I had for my personal safety.

The timing for this new crisis was less than perfect. It was deer hunting season. My husband grew up in a family of hunters. That year, Jennings and his brother rented a cabin in the Allegheny Mountains for weekend hunting during the season. There was no phone at the cabin, so I was unable to reach him when he was there and unless he called me, I had no lifeline. Basically, in an emergency, I was on my own.

I never really understood hunting. I hated guns. I never liked the concept of killing defenseless animals for sport. But in Pennsylvania, where my husband was raised, it was taken for granted that hunting was a part of manhood and it was a skill that was learned early by the young boys. Fathers and sons bonded in the snowy fields during deer season.

I remember we spent the first Thanksgiving after our reconciliation at his parents' farm in western Pennsylvania. It had been a beautiful winter week and the hills around the farm were covered with a blanket of crystal snow. Looking out the window, the pine trees beyond the clearing at the edge of the hills reminded me of green gumdrops plopped on white icing, randomly placed on the rolling hills.

That year, being back together again, we had so much to be thankful for and we stuffed ourselves with the bountiful foods that were prepared by his mother. Afterwards, we gathered by the fire for dessert of warm homemade apple pie; the aphrodisiac of the foods we had eaten still lingering about us.

"Thar' he goes, I saw five points on them antlers!", his father shouted as he and the other men leapt from their chairs and they were off; coats and hats flying in the air as they reached for their guns outside the kitchen door. The hunt was on.

Out of curiosity I got up and looked out the front window. The men were scattering over the hillside, leaving trails behind them in the snow, and then disappeared into the trees at the top of the hill. I looked, straining to see, but the hillside was empty. Good, I thought. Maybe he got away.

Then a sharp crack; then another. And then another in rapid succession. Crack. Crack. Crack. Echoing against the hills. The house became so quiet it was as if everyone in the room was taken down by those bullets; the women; the children. For a moment there was the stillness of death inside that house. I'll never forget the eerie feeling of it.

Transfixed at the window, I finally saw Jennings and his father drag the animal into the clearing. My husband had been the victor. I could see his father patting him on the back as if to say, "Well done, Son."

Jennings bent over the animal and I watched as warm vapor rose into the air above the men's heads, then a trail of red, fanning out, spilling onto the virgin snow. I had to turn away from the window and walk to where the children were playing quietly on the floor. I scooped my son up in my arms and held him close to me. I was beginning to realize that we sometimes love without knowing or understanding why. My husband and I had come from very different worlds, but I truly loved him in spite of our difficult beginnings.

It was hard for me to concentrate on my work with a demented fan out there somewhere that I knew could hurt me at any time. The pleasure I had getting up each morning and going to work; work that never seemed like work because I enjoyed it so, was slowly ending, being replaced by a dreadful, ominous sinking feeling in my stomach every morning.

Because of my situation, I was nervous about going out alone. This complicated my ability to meet the children's needs for activities on the weekends so I tried to schedule outings with them in very public places. During Jennings' absence I often took them skating at the indoor rink in town. It was a popular gathering place for most of their friends and I knew a few of the mothers who would be there, so it was also an outing for me.

One Saturday in mid-January we decided to spend the morning at the rink. It took a half an hour looking for lost mittens and matching boots. Skate sizes were sorted and tied together and finally we were off to the rink where the bundling process would be reversed; pulling and lacing three pairs of skates, undoing the lumps in the socks; laces too tight; too loose; ankles bending; others too tight. Whatever margin of error there was, I had to fix it.

Already spent before the morning had begun, I would run toward the snack bar and get my morning fix of caffeine, take my place on the benches around the rink with the other worn-out dutiful mothers and proudly watch my offspring giggle, glide and stumble around the rink. Sitting there, I realized how lucky I was and how much I loved my children. They were too young to appreciate it, but I would walk to the ends of the earth for them if I had to.

After the skating period was over, one by one they reluctantly returned to the bench where I was sitting and the unbundling-bundling process began all over again. After a bit of cranking and groaning, we walked out into a light dusting of snow. The children squealed as they practiced their snow sliding techniques on the slippery surface beneath their feet. I was grateful just to keep upright until I reached the car.

I quickly unlocked the doors and they piled in, one on top of another, pushing and playfully shoving to their seats. As I walked around to unlock my side, I realized my front left tire looked rather flat. Then I checked the back left tire to compare and it was completely flat. What luck, I thought as I went around to the passenger side of the car. They were all flat. I bent down to inspect them more closely and then had to convince myself that yes, all four of my tires had been slashed. Who would be sick enough to do this to me? The haunting reality of my demented admirer came into focus.

I immediately took the children back to the warmth and safety of the rink and called the garage to come and bring replacement tires with them. I bought them hot dogs and hot chocolate and tried to control my anger. The longer I sat there waiting for the truck, the greater my frustration and isolation became in not being able to contact my husband.

"We are going to have to tow you to the garage, Ma'am." the driver said. "What for? Can't you just change the tires here?" I questioned.

"It's not that easy," he replied, "the bolts have been tightened and stripped. All of them."

That meant towing the car to the garage with all of us piled in beside him on the front seat. The young man quickly attempted to clean the grimy seat of its litter and the children and I squeezed into the cab of the truck.

We huddled for the next two hours waiting our turn in a cold garage that smelled of automobile fluids and baloney and onion sandwiches while they worked on my car. 'Woe-is-me' country music was playing from the radio and the reality of what was happening to me was slowly sinking in. Maybe it was an act of random vandalism, but I strongly suspected that the gravel-voiced man had targeted me for either aggravation or extinction. Now I knew I was not even safe in public places. And worst of all, the safety of my children had been jeopardized. I wanted Jennings. I needed him around me and not so far away. More than ever I couldn't be left alone. Somehow we had to restructure our lives so that we could find this man who was terrorizing me.

Jennings arrived home just before sunset that night and after the children were in bed, I related what had happened to us at the skating rink. His face was intent, marking my every word as I went through the details of the incident. I could barely get the story out and the lump in my throat constricted my words as I choked back tears. He held me tightly in his arms. "I'm here now. I won't let that son-of-a-bitch hurt you. Nothing's going to happen to you as long as I'm around. You have my word." And I believed with all my heart that he would protect me.

My husband was truly a dichotomy in the history of our relationship. At times so loving; at others, so emotionally removed. I wanted to believe in him as my protector. I had no one else. I needed to trust his judgment when he said we shouldn't go to the police with our suspicions. That could generate unwanted publicity and encourage the stalker to be more aggressive. He assured me that he wouldn't go hunting on weekends anymore and would spend his time at home with us. I had to depend upon Jennings, my only ally against my enemy.

Over the next few weeks, Jennings kept his promise and stayed home on weekends and I tried not to spend as much time at work by doing some of my research at home. After a few weeks, I began to relax and almost convinced myself that the tire incident had been a random act of vandalism. But the calm didn't last long.

As was my habit, I had driven to the station early in the morning to prepare for my afternoon show. Usually, I would be on my way home after finishing the six o'clock news, but that day I was taping a late interview with Pierre Salinger who had young Teddy Kennedy in tow. Mr.

Salinger and his entourage were running a little late, so by the time I wrapped that evening it was close to ten o'clock.

My producer walked me to my car and waited until I pulled out of the parking lot. I reached over and turned on the heat and then clicked on the radio as I wound down the hill from the station and onto the main road, heading south. I was feeling tired, but rather elated at what I felt was a good interview. I was running through my head the editing I would do tomorrow on the piece. Intellectually, Mr. Salinger was an interesting subject, but I began to speculate on this younger Kennedy and what his future might hold. Certainly the Kennedy name had power connected to it, but other than good looks, I couldn't get much substance in off-camera chats with Ted Kennedy. I personally didn't feel that he had the same dynamics his older brother John had, but I was convinced that with his handsome face he probably could get elected if he ran for office. Others with lesser connections have won elections on looks alone and with the Kennedy name, he would have few challengers.

Then, of course, my mind became preoccupied with thoughts about Ted Kennedy and the Chappaquidick accident where Mary Jo drowned and Ted allegedly swam away. Supposedly, he left her there, imprisoned in the car he had driven into the water.

Then all of a sudden an unusual smell caught my attention. What is it? It's just the heater, I guessed. As I continued driving, the odor, a chemical smell of some sort, became stronger. As I turned off the heater, I glanced at the dashboard to see if any warning lights were on. I noticed my cigarette lighter was pushed in. How did that happen, I wondered? I have never even used the darn thing. I reached over and tried to disengage the lighter, but I couldn't; it appeared to be stuck. I pulled harder to no avail. I touched the top of the dashboard above the lighter and it felt hot.

I wasn't sure how hot the dash would have to get to combust, but I didn't want to take any chances. Just ahead I saw an exit sign on the dark freeway. I had to chance that there would be a service station nearby where I could get help. I pressed on the accelerator to reach the exit faster. For once I wished there were a state trooper around as I hit 85 mph on my speedometer.

The five miles seemed like twenty. I slowed down as I neared the exit and carefully managed the sharp turn off the freeway onto the country road. It was dark. Nothing was in sight. Left? Or should I turn right? I flipped a coin in my head and turned left and prayed it was the right decision. I rolled down the window a little bit, just enough to keep out the cold, yet release the noxious odor of smoldering wire. My eyes searched the darkness for some sign of life. Then I saw lights of a town in the distance and on the edge of the road ahead, a high Texaco sign beamed down at me. By now the smell of burning was beginning to make me nauseous and I rolled the window all the way down. I screeched into the station and almost knocked over the cans of oil stacked neatly by the pumps as I pulled up near the garage doors.

"Hey, lady, what's your hurry?" the attendant yelled angrily, ready to let me have all the expletives in his vocabulary. I jumped out of the car that was by this time starting to smoke. "Holy crap! You're car's smoking. You'll blow this whole damn station up. Get outa' the way, he hollered as he pushed me aside and ran toward the station.

In two seconds he was back with a fire extinguisher. I stood there shaking as he sprayed under the hood with white chemical foam. Someone else came running with a large hammer ready to bash in my dash, but the attendant had it under control. And it was over. I got back in the car, locked the doors and drove away in a daze.

Now I could no longer dismiss the acts of violence. They were not accidental or random. The next time maybe it wouldn't just involve my car; it would involve me. Or even more horrendous, my children. I went to bed that night in the comfort of my husband's arms, replaying the day's events over and over again in my mind. The fear would not go away and sleep was impossible. I didn't know how I could face another day at work knowing my hunter was out there watching my every move. Who knew how vigilant this demented person would continue to be in his campaign to do me bodily harm.

Jennings instilled into my head that we should keep these incidences as quiet as possible and work though private channels to find my stalker. He knew a retired detective, he said who he could get to take it on. Jennings assured me that if he couldn't help us, then we would go to the police. Just leave it to him, he said.

My husband's contact started on the case immediately. He had little to go on except for the details of the events leading up to the car fire. He would investigate and search every angle for someone the area with a background that could match the behavior of my stalker. From my investigative work as a reporter, I knew he would have access to information that would encompass files and other sources within the prison system. I highly suspected my stalker was a fan from prison that was now on the streets. In the meantime, I went about my work trying to act as normally as possible when, in truth, I was living in a constant state of fear that all but paralyzed me.

The strain also seemed to be taking a toll on Jennings. Somewhere deep within me I knew I was being selfish to continue to draw my family into this precarious situation, all because I worked in the public eye. Was it really worth it?

Within weeks I had my answer. One morning before we were to leave the house, Jennings discovered that the wires on our car battery had been crossed. A chill ran through me. I was not safe anywhere, any time, anymore. Not even in my own home. My enemy who was determined to love me to death would not stop until his goal was completed. And in the process, my family could be harmed as well. The reality of what was happening to me was never clearer nor my choice of what had to be done more definite.

The next morning, I handed in my notice from the job that was so fulfilling for me, and so many would have given their eyeteeth to have. But now, as far as I was concerned, nothing else mattered, my dream career had to end. Whatever life my husband and I had built, we would have to leave it behind and find a haven far away from public life and the violence that was inevitable for me if I continued my career. I didn't see that I had any other choice.

12

Jennings sold his partnership in his alloy factory and found a management job in the New Jersey shore area. Until we settled in, I had not had time to stop and contemplate the changes all of us were making in our lives. I only knew that I felt safer far away from the demon that was after me.

For the first time, too, I began to realize the emotional toll my stalker had taken on me. I was tired, both mentally and physically. The stress of living on the edge emotionally for so long had been wearing on me and it didn't take me long to see the positive side of my decision to leave my career. I realized that although it was a choice that was forced upon me, in the long run, my being able to spend more of my day with the children was the best medicine for all of us. As much as I missed being in the center of things, I knew my children needed me and deserved to have me as a full-time mother.

Before I knew, a year had gone by, then another. The children were growing up and they and Jennings had anchored themselves securely into their new environment. Jennings became a Deacon in our church and we, as a family, attended most of the church functions.

It was just about three years into our move to New Jersey that Jennings began to take weekend trips to go hunting during deer season with his brother. He had made so many adjustments in his life because of my circumstances, that although I didn't like being alone on weekends, I tried to understand his need to touch base with his roots once in awhile. And in reality, I still hated hunting and also still felt nervous about wandering about in the environment that represented danger to me. But, eventually, the loneliness during his trips away from home began eating away at me.

It was Friday afternoon and Jennings was packing for another one of his hunting trips, this time with a friend from work. They were both to drive to the mountains where they were to meet up with my husband's brother at his cabin in the mountains. I didn't want to be left alone again with no way to reach him, but he was determined to go.

"Come, give Daddy a hug, little guy," Jennings called from the front doorway as he was preparing to leave. Our toddler ran across the room from where he had been playing. As he passed the couch, his unsteady little foot caught on the edge of the rug and he lost his balance and was thrust head long against the sharp edge of the coffee table.

None of us were quick enough to stop Lee's fall. I could hear the sickening thud of his forehead as he hit the table and rolled to the floor, stunned by the blow. I rushed over to him and picked his limp body up off of the floor. I could see blood gushing from his forehead and running into his left eye. I put my hand over the wound and applied pressure to help stop the bleeding, but it was almost impossible because he was past being stunned and was now screaming and struggling to get out of my arms.

Jennings hadn't moved from his place in the doorway. His bag was still in his hand. "Please stay, " I said. Then I remember him giving me a lecture on how minor head wounds bleed excessively and that he had to run, but would call me from a pay phone when he got there. "Just this once," I begged him. He walked out the door as if he had never heard me and left me standing, holding our son's bleeding head.

The plastic surgeon put ten stitches in his "nothing to worry about" gash and I drove back from the hospital that afternoon, determined that I had had enough. I waited up that night for a call from Jennings. I waited all weekend, but he never called home to see how Lee was. That was the final straw for me. At least I could look for a job and insure myself the independence that comes with having my own income. That way, when Jennings wasn't around, I would have something else to occupy my mind and give me an added sense of fulfillment outside of our home.

With my background, I had no trouble finding employment. Monday morning I set about looking for work without telling anyone and within a week I accepted a job as media director for a company specializing in media product for children.

When Jennings came home from his trip, I told him I had decided to go back to work. I knew he was happier since I had given up my career, but I never predicted the degree he would carry out his anger on my decision to go back to work. Especially without consulting him. Jennings just looked at me with a steady glare in his eyes and defiantly walked toward me. He pointed his finger in my face, "I warn you, just make sure your high fluten' job doesn't interfere with the welfare of my son." And he walked out of the room. I had not seen that look since the night years ago when I rejected his advances.

Isaac Newton must have been doing his research looking through my back door. What goes up, must come down. After about a week on my new job, the phone rang in my office and my secretary informed me I had a call.

"Hello, Ms. Hart, It's been a long time. How are you. I've missed you."

My blood ran cold. I never could forget that voice. It was him. He had found me. Terror gripped my whole being as I stood there speechless; the phone receiver frozen in my hand. The overwhelming enormity of what was happening again burned into my brain and my heart began to pound wildly in my chest. What should I do? I couldn't tell anyone at work. Jennings was still so angry with me for taking this job. How could I depend on him to have any sympathy for me? I regretted being so cocky with him and burning my bridges.

The phone rang again. I stared at the phone. It rang once. Then silence. Then another steady ring; then nothing. The door opened and I jumped. It was my secretary.

"Mrs. Hart, I rang you but you didn't pick up. It's that same man again. He said he had accidentally been cut off and he wanted to talk to you about fire insurance, or something."

Our house! He knows where I live. I grabbed my coat and ran out of the building and got into my car. I had forgotten about my own welfare and didn't even consider there could have been a bomb wired to it. I was only thinking of my children. I just had to get home to protect my family.

Our house was on a three-acre cul du sac. Our road only had six houses on it and there was a slight incline at the road's entrance before it started to gently slope down toward our house. As I entered the short road, our place was not yet visible. I was praying all the way. The nose of my car edged up and then down again as I reached the crescent of the hill.

I could see the house. Everything looked okay. As I got closer I saw the girls playing in the front under the trees with some friends. I turned into the driveway and heard the crunch of the small beach stones beneath the wheels of my car. I was still frightened, but I felt safer now that I was home.

The children came running up to me and I gave them a big hug. "Gee, Mom, not so hard. You're squeezing me to death," Alison squealed before scampering off to resume playing with their friends. Brett tilted her head as though to demand an immediate response, "Why are you home?"

"It's a surprise. Get your sister and tell your friends you'll see them later."

"Sounds fishy to me. What kind of surprise?" my ten-year-old prodded, "Tell me first, I won't tell."

I was losing my patience with her. "Now! Get your sister and come into the house."

She walked away grumbling how mean I was being, but did what she was told and we quickly went into the house together to find my husband.

Jennings and Lee were in the living room watching an old John Wayne western and they hadn't heard us come in. He turned away from the screen when he heard the girls. "Why home so early? Get fired?" His attitude was less than receptive in seeing me. I would have a hard time telling my story.

I took the children into the kitchen and gave them ice cream and cookies and told them I had to talk to Daddy about something.

Jennings was still watching television when I returned to the living room.

"He called today."

"Who called today?"

"My stalker. He called me at work."

Jennings didn't move from his chair and I waited, holding my breath for his response.

Then it came. "I don't know whether I can go through this again with you, Sandra. Honestly I don't."

The floor could have fallen out from beneath me and swallowed me up and I wouldn't have cared. The physical threats my stalker could impose upon me could be no worse than the emotional torture I was going through fearing my husband's abandonment. Once again I was standing in front of the mirror, bruised and emotionally broken, only this time there may not be a second chance. My ego was fraying. I didn't want to beg; to let him know how weak I had become. I put my hand to my face to shield my emotions; hold back the tears. But they came in spite of my efforts.

Jennings must have risen from his chair. I felt his arms surround my body and he gently kissed the top of my head. "Don't cry, I'm not going anywhere. You're stuck with me for life, Kiddo. I'll call Pittsburgh tomorrow and see what we can do. In the meantime, I'll get my rifle out and make sure it's in a safe place away from the children and where I can get to it if I need it. I don't think that guy will come around as long he knows you're not alone."

My hatred of guns made me wary of having a rifle in the house. Jennings was careful enough not to have it loaded. But in spite of that precaution, I still remembered how many times on my news broadcasts I had reported killings that had occurred when the victim's weapon was used against them.

The crazed animal knew where I worked. And probably where I lived. I was a prisoner of my circumstances again. Jennings once more would have the burden of my problems. I decided to carry on as best I could at work. Although it was a false sense of security, I honestly felt safer there than at home. I didn't believe that he would harm me in an office filled with people. Plus when I was at work, the stress of my children's safety was partially removed.

The investigator called and had his men working on reopening the investigation. One request was for us to have both phones at home and work tapped. Of course that meant bringing my boss into my problems. The next morning, behind closed doors, I relayed my tale of terror to the owner of the company. He seemed sympathetic and told us there would be no problem with the investigator's plans to tap my office line. Arrangements were made to have the work done the next day.

That night my boss called me at home and said not to come in. He feared for his other employees, he said. They would send a severance check. I was terminated. I wasn't surprised. Another decision made for me. First, my husband would be assured I was no longer employed and that would make him happy. Secondly, the stalker would know right where I was all the time and that would be convenient for him. All of the men in my life had me right where they wanted me. I was prepared for the worst.

My thoughts went back again to Pittsburgh and the fears I had then. If he were to strike I hope that his only wish was to get me and not my children. If it had to be, let him only take me.

13

As the days of my mental imprisonment turned into weeks, I began pacing the rooms of my home like a caged animal. The notes the investigator asked me to write, trying to dredge up any past facts that might prove to be a lead, became a daily burden, as it forced me to constantly be reminded that someone was out there wanting to torture me. Finally, in one of my darkest moments, I threw my notes into the fireplace and lit a match to them. No longer the rock I had always thought myself to be, I slowly was coming apart. I was snapping at my children at the smallest upset and unmerciful toward my husband. I secretly resented his freedom and my need to be bound to him for my safety. Just to be able to drive to the beach alone or go to the country store nearby for the morning newspaper, small pleasures I took for granted, now were excursions of fear.

Night and day I could not shake the fear of doom I felt inside. My months of being bedridden with rheumatic fever came back to haunt me again. In dreams I relived the pain and the loneliness my childhood illness brought me. I would hover over my young image, small and white, lying in the center of a big bed that was even whiter. The walls of the room were dark and high and there were no windows. I could hear voices of happy children outside the room, but I was never able to hear what they were saying, and my body would feel as heavy as though a powerful invisible force was holding me down. Although I struggled, I couldn't get out of bed. I would wake up each time after this nightmare in a cold sweat. I was ashamed of my weakness and could not share it with anyone, especially my husband. The constant reality that unless my stalker was caught, he would be back someday and it could be over.

The stress on all of us was enormous. Jennings started complaining about pains in his chest. He would lie in bed unable to sleep convinced he was having a heart attack. Our doctor said it was stress. Our circumstances were taking toll on both of us. He would call me four or five times during the day, and if I didn't answer, he would come home to check to see if everything was okay. He was beginning to be as obsessive as I was.

One evening in early November, Jennings was working late, the children were in bed, and I was watching the evening news. I thought I heard sounds outside near the window. It could be a raccoon, I thought. They had been getting into our garbage for months and no matter how we tried to secure the lids to the cans, those smart little creatures were able to open them and spill the garbage all along the side of the house.

But the noise became louder. It sounded like human steps walking through the leaves on the walkway. The sound was magnified a thousand times by my sudden terror. My hand trembled as I turned off the living room light and carefully peered out of the window. I couldn't see anything. Should I call the police? What should I do? My mind was playing tricks on me. The moment I had replayed over and over in my mind had come and I was still thinking about raccoons or embarrassing myself with a false alarm.

I crawled across the floor to the kitchen on my hands and knees in the darkness and groped for the phone on the table. My hand slipped on the slick tile floor and thrust my body forward into the glass tabletop, it's corner slicing through my upper lip. I felt the pain of the instant impact, but I was more concerned with the noise I was making that would identify my location in the house. It was not until I felt the warm, sanguine fluid in my mouth that I realized I had been cut. I couldn't remember the number for our local police, for months etched clearly in my mind, now it was lost. I dialed the operator and she put me through.

"This is Mrs. Hart, I heard a noise outside and I think someone is there. Please come and check. I'm alone." I tried to hide my terror as I spoke to the dispatcher. I ignored the blood that was warming my chin and trickling down my neck. I gave them the address and waited.

I kept the lights off so that I could move about the house without anyone seeing me. I grabbed a kitchen towel and pressed it against my wound and tried to keep my head up as I moved down the hall to check on the children. I sat on the floor, my senses sharpened by my raging adrenaline, listening for the crash of breaking window glass or knobs turning, watching intently for the lights of the squad car to reflect off the wall in the children's room.

Within minutes, I saw the bright headlights of the police car. They put a search light on the house and moved it about the yard. I got up and carefully peered out the window. I saw two officers get out of the car and split up. One was heading for my front door and the other was going around the backside of the house. Each of them held flashlights which they were shining around as they walked. I heard the officer in the back call to the other officer heading quickly for our front door. In a moment there was a loud knock. I turned on the porch light and saw one of the officers. My lip was pulsing, but had stopped bleeding by the time I opened the door. The officer started to say something when he saw the blood, but I quickly showed him my lip and explained. I was sure at that point that I had humiliated myself with a hyperactive imagination over a bunch of raccoons, until he spoke.

"There's a white male out here that is in distress. He's lying on the ground and needs immediate attention. My partner has radioed for the paramedics. Would you mind coming out here to see if you recognize him?"

A mixture of fear and self-vindication was running thought my veins as I went outside with the officer and walked to the place where a man dressed in a worn leather jacket was lying face up on the ground. I was not prepared for what next met my eyes. It was Jennings.

I spoke through a mouth that was beginning to swell and throb painfully; identifying the man as my husband as I kneeled down beside him. He didn't respond. Maybe he had a stroke, I thought as I touched his motionless form, cradled by the dry leaves on the pathway.

I ran back into the house and grabbed a blanket from the couch and covered him. Just then I heard the ambulance pull into the driveway. I threw a raincoat over my bloodstained shirt, woke the children and I scooped them into the car and we all headed for the hospital. As I drove, I prayed that my husband would be okay.

Jennings was taken directly to the emergency room of our community hospital where he was monitored. The doctors weren't sure what was wrong with him and wanted to admit him for further tests. They told me I couldn't help him and that it would be better for me to go home and get some sleep. They tended to my cut lip and then released me. I left the hospital not knowing what was going to be next. I honestly didn't know how much more I could take. I felt so sorry for my children who had been drawn into all of through no action of their own. They were just along for the ride of my life. It was so unfair to them to be swept up in a journey that was so unpredictable with no end in sight. A journey whose outcome none of us could control.

Driving home that night I felt as though I had been set out to sea with my fate at the will of the winds. Whatever direction they were blowing, that is where I would go. If something happened to my husband, I hadn't the slightest clue as to what I would do with my life.

Jennings had extensive tests done on him during the week he was in the hospital and at the end of his stay, his attending physician called me in to meet with him. He said that tests indicated his motor reflexes are normal and he had regained the use of his legs. "We really have not been able to find anything physically wrong with him."

"How can that be? How could he be paralyzed and not have had a stroke or something?" I didn't understand what he was trying to tell me.

Then he dropped the bombshell. "Well, your husband's mental illness has predisposed him to psychosomatic symptoms that are real to the patient and at the same time can also produce results such as chest pains mimicking a heart attack or, in severe cases like Mr. Hart's, psychosomatic paralysis."

I was totally confused, "What do you mean, 'his mental condition'?"

"His schizophrenia."

The doctor's words hit me like a brick. Was he talking about the same man that I knew? I couldn't believe it. There must be some mistake. "I'm sorry, you must be mistaken."

He started nervously shuffling the papers he had on his desk, "I assumed as his wife you knew. His records we sent for from Pennsylvania, indicate he was treated for schizophrenia in the past."

There was an uncomfortable silence in the room as I was computing this new information that had entered into my life. I knew Jennings had been in therapy while we were separated, but he told me it was to work out issues that involved my leaving him.

"He has schizophrenia?" I heard myself break the silence by putting those words together, hoping I misunderstood him.

"Yes," he confirmed. "And it is important that you understand the seriousness of his illness, because he is in a state of acute paranoia and we will have to try to get him stabilized with medication before we can release him."

The doctor then continued by asking me various questions about Jennings' personality from my perspective; his habits, or if he displayed an unusual behavior toward me.

The way I looked at it, considering my life so far, I was not the one to judge what was "normal" and what was not. Too much high drama was going on around me constantly. I would be the last person to be able to qualify normal behavior. At that point, I didn't think I had ever seen or would be able to recognize "normal" if I had. I knew Jennings would exaggerate the truth sometimes, but a lot of people did that. He wanted to be more than he really was. His white lies made him feel good about himself and I ignored them.

I sat there in the doctor's office that morning, feeling a lot of things and asking myself the same questions that I would ask myself over and over again in the ensuing years. How is it possible that I, supposedly an intelligent woman, didn't suspect his condition? Was I so concerned about myself that I didn't see? Who would believe that someone could live with a man eight years and not know.

"Why didn't I realize?" I said out loud, more to myself than the doctor.

"For one thing, you may be too close to the situation," he said. "As a wife you may have accepted certain behavior that others would find not acceptable. Like having a child who throws temper tantrums. You love that child in spite of his behavior, unconditionally. Not always approving, yet condoning certain behavior you necessarily will ever accept from anyone else. Secondly, paranoid schizophrenics are usually very good at, well, does the phrase, 'cunning like a fox' help? Don't quote me on that, but it might help you to understand what I mean."

Unfortunately I did. Hindsight can be a great teacher and I had a feeling I had old and new lessons to learn in the months to come. I wasn't sure I was up to it.

I spent an hour that day going over my husband's behavior patterns as much as I could. The doctor suggested several books that I could get that would help me learn more about schizophrenia and how it works on the mind. He thought that with medication and outpatient psychotherapy, my husband's condition could be stabilized.

Jennings finally was released from the hospital and he seemed to be quite eager to resume work again. In the ensuing weeks, he acted as though nothing had happened, but I had changed. I was having trouble forgetting that he never was honest with me from the start about his illness.

The more I learned about schizophrenia the more the pieces of the puzzle started coming together. His constant checking on me, the earlier phone calls that were supposed to be concerns for my safety, all now had deeper meaning. He was only worried that I was out of his control. Little lies and exaggerations that before just annoyed, now had a new importance to them. I had little faith in anything he told me. Perhaps I was taking it to the extreme, but ignorance is not bliss. What I did not know or suspect about my husband's condition was a dangerous and destructive ignorance. In my case, my husband's motives and his actions were now being questioned by me. In a way, I guess, some of his paranoia was rubbing off on me. I became suspicious that his actions may have always had a veiled motive.

About three weeks into my husband's therapy, his psychiatrist called and said that he wanted to see me. When I came into his office the doctor started to ask me questions about my fidelity to my husband. He more or less intimated that Jennings had told him that I had been unfaithful to him and that I was a big part of his paranoia. I needed another man in my life like I needed the plague. Jennings had convinced himself and freely told all who would listen that I was an unfaithful wife. He had transferred his paranoia to me, the only one in the world who tried to love him. I was now the target of his delusions.

The first doctor had been right. Jennings had the ability to fantasize just about anything and make it seem real, at least to him. He was believable and just might be smart enough to get his way by making people think that I was the one with the problem. I didn't know what tactic to follow next. Should I confront Jennings about his fears and try to ease his paranoia or should I choose to hide behind my anger and suffer? Would it really matter? Could I reach beyond his insanity and touch some area of reason within him? Would I be treading into dangerous territory that could trigger his paranoia into a weapon of violence against me? I was torn between reason and a compelling force to confront my husband with his lies. The situation was both frightening and hopeless. There was no doubt he was consumed by a fantasy world unknown to the rest of us. He had scripted the play and given us parts that we had to flesh out. In his mind there was no other way it could be. If I were to stay with him, it was a role I would have to play.

I had failed in my first marriage because I gave up too quickly. I was young and hungry to taste life. I didn't want to make the same mistake again, uproot my family and start all over if there was a chance that Jennings could get well. Perhaps the best answer was to keep the family as stable as I could for the sake of the children. I didn't know what I was going to do.

During the ride home, I looked into my rear view mirror and noticed the same blue van had been behind me since I pulled out of the hospital parking lot. I didn't concern myself, until after enough turns, I realized it was still following me. Couldn't be, I thought. I really can't handle any more stress now. I am becoming paranoid, I scolded myself. I looked again and mentally copied down the license plate number, just in case. I decided I would change the way I usually went home and I started to take other, old familiar roads, hoping the van just happened to be someone going my way and not intentionally following me. But no matter where I turned, the van was still right behind me. He *was* following me. There was no doubt about that now. I slowed down a little bit to see if I could make out the driver's face. He was too far away. I could only see that it was a man in a baseball cap.

This time, I didn't even think twice about what to do. I knew that I didn't want to go straight home, so I headed toward my local police station. As I drove, the van continued right along behind me, keeping a safe distance, but when I made a right into the police station, instead of climbing the steep hill to my house, the van quickly veered left and drove out of sight, speeding away in the opposite direction. I sat there for a moment and breathed a sigh of relief.

My knees felt unsure as I descended the few steps to the police department that was housed in the basement of the borough's municipal building. In a town that is only one square mile and has little over 1,200 residential homes, it was hard to be invisible. I was sure that word had gone around town about the incident with Jennings outside the house that night and my bloody lip, so it was with a mixture of caution and embarrassment that I entered the doors and asked to speak to someone.

The detective in charge came out and filed a report on the incident. He didn't seem to think I was crazy or at least, if he did, he hid it well. He promised to follow up as soon a possible and get back to me if he found out anything. An officer followed me home and after checking around the house, he said he would patrol the area several times a day until his superior had news about the driver of the van.

What else could happen? I tried not to show my fear in front of my children. But this time I was really being pushed over the edge. I didn't know how much more I could stand. But the biggest weight that I bore was the concern of what all this was doing to my children.

A few hours later the phone rang. The detective had found out who was following me and Jennings was responsible. I couldn't believe what I was hearing.

So many questions were swirling around in my head as I hung up the phone. I stood there momentarily, just staring at nothing, when my eyes focused on a wire leading from the telephone and running directly into the bottom of the refrigerator through the grill. It was pushed out at a slight angle.

The pieces of the puzzle were falling into place. I got down on my knees and tried to pry open the grill. It came off easily and I bent my head down to see if I could tell what was attached to the wire. I reached my hand under the refrigerator and pulled out a device of some kind. On further inspection, I saw it was a tape recorder. I was both outraged and frightened. This had to be the work of a very sick man.

First the shock of finding out that Jennings had hired someone to follow me, and then to wonder how long had he been recording my conversations? He still was convinced that I was seeing another man and he had been having me followed every time I left the house. How could I have been so blind as not to see? It was just a coincidence that I looked into my rear view mirror at the right time. Who was this crazy, paranoid being that took over my husband's body?

These final discoveries were the breaking point. I couldn't take it any longer. The mountain finally crumbled. I knelt there, my body refusing to release the pain welling up inside me. The anger that had been bottled inside of me for so long refused to be released. There I was, on my knees, trembling, so deeply immersed in my pain that I didn't see my young son come up behind me. It was not until he wrapped his little arms around my head to comfort me that I even realized that he was there. I turned and held him in my arms. "Mommy's okay." I assured him.

I didn't know what to do next. I knew I couldn't stay with Jennings. After the discovery of the recorder, I was determined that I would no longer be his victim and I had to protect myself as well as my family. No matter the cost. I replaced the device as best I could, the way I found it. I was afraid of Jennings and I didn't want him to know I was on to him. It wasn't time yet. I had to have my plans set as to what I was going to do.

My mind started framing my moves as if maneuvering in a game of chess. I knew it wouldn't be too long before the man in the van would have to confront my husband with the fact that he had been caught. I was counting on the driver being afraid to tell him right away that he had confessed to the police and had implicated him. If so, we would be safe for a little while longer. Jennings had been his most powerful player in his game with me and I had to bring him into checkmate before it was too late.

The next day, after Jennings went to work and the children were at school, I drove to a peaceful wooded park near our house. I have always loved the outdoors and when I am around nature, my head clears and I can think better. Maybe it is the connection with things that are given life over and over again; a new chance to grow taller or blossom more beautifully or to fly about the universe with untethered wings.

I parked my car and strolled down toward the bridal path my children and I often took, then wound around through the trees. It was so peaceful. I picked up a strong, straight branch from the ground that begged for walking, broke off the weak side branches and used it to support my steps on the frozen ground.

The dirt was dimpled with rivets where horses' hooves had tattooed the ground. As I made my way through the naked trees, I began to relax a little. I could hear the birds above me singing their winter songs. I wrapped my muffler around my neck a little more securely and continued along the trail until I came out onto a clearing. I could feel the short grass crunch beneath my feet, dry from the winter's cold and I found a log at the edge of the clearing that had weathered the abuses of hooves not clearing it's girth.

I sat on the battered old log and looked out over the expanse before me and I thought about my life for a long while. I thought about all the years with Jennings; the happy times; the darker times. The trauma I had gone through with him; finding him with another woman; having our child alone; giving up a career that I loved. All of this seemed so surreal, as if it belonged to some else's life. Not mine. It couldn't belong to the little girl from Ohio with big dreams for her life.

I recalled reading something written by Eleanor Roosevelt I had read during the time I lived in New York. She wrote that we..." gain strength, courage and confidence by every experience in which you really stop to look fear in the face. You are able to say to yourself, I lived through this horror. I can take the next thing that comes along. You must do the thing you cannot do." That passage never had so much relevance to me as it did while sitting on that log on that clear winter's day.

I got up from my comfortable resting spot and continued to walk across the clearing and took the trail that doubled back to where I had started. I walked up the grassy slope to my car and drove home, still not able to see my future.

It seemed strange to me, but in spite of all that had happened in the past months, I found myself with a very bizarre sense of freedom and power that I hadn't felt in a long time. I now only had one demon to exorcise from my life; my husband. I had to face the painful truth that Jennings and my stalker were one and the same. Powered by his paranoia; his schizophrenia; it had been Jennings all those years. I knew what I had to do. I prayed that God would give me the strength.

14

I have since learned, being married to a paranoid schizophrenic for so many years, I had eventually become a perfect example of cognitive neoassociation. Trauma and violence that I had experienced in my life with Jennings obliterated my other mental functions, rendering me unable to concentrate on anything but the images of dysfunction in my life. During those years of extreme stress, I was subject to a neurological numbness by the things that were happening to me. Although I appeared to be functioning on a normal level on the surface, internally I could not see things as they really were.

To paraphrase Woodrow Wilson, on his comments after viewing D. W. Griffith's *Birth Of A Nation*, my reaction the events in my life is similar, when I say that putting my memories of Jennings down on paper is like writing with lightning. And my only regret is that it is all so terribly true.

It took a long time for me to admit defeat. It was hard for me to accept failure, but the time had come in my marriage, the point at which I knew I would have to stop beating my head against a brick wall. I had to let go, but I knew Jennings would not be so willing as to let me freely walk out of his life alive. My fate was in the hands of a higher force to show me the way. I didn't have to wait long. It came that evening.

Up to this point, Jennings had suspected nothing. Evidently the van driver never confessed to Jennings that he had been caught following me. As far as my husband knew, I was completely in the dark.

The girls were sleeping over at a friend's house that evening, so after dinner I took over their chores by clearing the table and cleaning the kitchen. I gave my son a bath and put him to bed, a hard task now that he was growing up and being scrubbed clean in a bathtub wasn't a priority. I thought about how quickly the years had flown away from me, the dragon of time belching flames, burning away the years.

Jennings was watching the news and I excused myself and went to bed. I replayed in my mind for the hundredth time my plans to escape tomorrow. Escape back to my parents' in Ohio.

Just as I was about to fall into a deep sleep, I felt Jennings' hot breath against my face, accusing, rambling words coming from deep within his throat. Accusing me of the worst acts of infidelity in incoherent sentences. He grabbed my arm and twisted it behind my back and I couldn't move. I screamed for him to let me go. I tried to struggle and free myself from beneath his body to no avail. I knew I was going to die, but I was not going to go without a fight. Then just a quickly as he attacked me, he released me and turned to walk away. He moved across the room toward the door as if to leave, then he suddenly turned around and lunged at me on the bed, his powerful six foot, muscular body ready to crush the life from me.

Looking back, I can't imagine the part of my being that overtook my body that last night with Jennings. I have never seen her again. But this force within me, this instinct for survival gave me the strength to fight back as I had never fought before. My repressed anger surfaced and all of the primal instincts of survival were armed against my predator. The stories I had reported as an anchorwoman. Headlines that I had read so objectively about domestic violence and murder. This one won't have my name on it. I would no longer be a victim. He had used my compassion against me and I had played right into his hands. I couldn't take it anymore. I wouldn't take it anymore. I wouldn't back down again. I had to stand up to him and pay the price no matter what the cost.

I quickly rolled from the edge of the bed onto the floor. My adrenaline was raging. I stood up, grabbed the mattress handles, and with all the strength I could gather lifted him and the mattress high enough and thrust him off the bed, his body slamming against the wall in a crumpled heap.

I ran out of the room to my son's bedroom down the hall and quickly locked the door behind me. I had little time before Jennings would come after me. I barricaded the door by sliding a dresser in front of it. My heart was racing, but somehow I was able to dial for help. I sat down in the rocking chair next to my son's bed. He was sleeping peacefully and the cadence of his breathing quieted my mind. I had cornered myself and was easy prey for my hunter. There were no other options. I sat in silence, made peace with God and waited.

Jennings never came. Unknown to me, the force of the impact had temporarily stunned Jennings and when the police arrived, he was sitting quietly and gave no resistance. Only God knows, but He did give me the strength to protect myself and saved me from being killed that night.

I didn't press charges and the police convinced Jennings to commit himself to a psychiatric hospital for treatment. Jennings was in the acute stages of schizophrenia and jail was not the answer.

I wish I could say that this is the end of the story and that Jennings got well and that we lived happily after. But it was too late. It was not meant to be.

When he was allowed visitors, I went to see Jennings in the hospital. We sat in his sparsely furnished room; husband and wife at the end of our journey together.

"You know, I really don't belong here," he said bending close to me in what was almost a whisper. Then he hissed, "You're the guilty one. You can tell me the truth now, they can't hear."

He got up and walked over to the wall and proudly showed me where he had stuffed a sheet of stationery over the intercom in his room. When he turned to look at me, there were tears in his eyes. "You know, I love you so much, I can't live without you." And he fell to his knees in front of me and looked up. "If I can't have you no one will."

With those words, a macabre sense of pity for him overcame me. Jennings had been a part of me for a long time. I had caressed his handsome face, laid next to his strong body, but the eye of his mind was beyond my grasp; locked away somewhere foreign to me. I knew his face, I knew his body, but I didn't know his mind. Perhaps even for him on his more lucid days, his thought processes that traveled far beyond the reaches of comprehension remained a deep, dark and impenetrable mystery. I longed to know the 'why' of it all, but there was no 'why'; it just was. I had to accept it. I never went back.

During the months he was in treatment, he escaped several times an returned toward the house, but luckily his absence at the hospital was discovered in time for him to be picked up and returned behind locked doors until he was well enough to be discharged.

After his treatment was completed he was released into the custody of his family in Pennsylvania and I started proceedings for a divorce. I was a victim of spousal abuse, but because I was still alive, the law wasn't on my side. He would have had to hurt me physically or kill me for the protective laws to be activated. Not even a legal document would ever stop him from following me or killing me, if he wanted. I knew that.

I went to work every day knowing that most days Jennings was out there somewhere watching me. But as long as he kept his distance and didn't hurt me, I couldn't do a thing about it. It was the '70's and there were no stalking laws to protect me. I was resigned that this was to be my life forever. Imprisoned without bars, caged by my life's choices.

15

And so it is that I finally come to the end of the chapters in my life with my second husband. Today it is as though Jennings Hart walked into and out of my life as a ghost. Because of his illness, his persona has been difficult to put on paper. He had so many hidden personalities.

In writing my memoir, being able to have a clear, well-defined picture of the person he was, even after all these years is elusive. His character is impossible to define precisely, because he allowed no one into his paranoia. He was a shadow in my life that took many shapes and has left me with only confused memories of Jennings and who he really was.

In my recollections, unfortunately, I can't get a true feel of him. I can only work with the facts about Jennings as I know them today. This ultimate mystery still amazes and saddens me, and perhaps was one of the motivations for this all to be written.

The man that I married wove separate tales and created different scenarios for each of his women. He was the rough macho man for the sexy bar fly; the sophisticated successful businessman for the upscale woman. He would attend the ballet, then just as easily shift gears and hang in seedy bars and sweet talk a woman over a beer or two.

After I separated from Jennings, I found out that at the time I was dating him, Jennings was still married and had only gotten divorced days before our marriage. And to complicate matters, he was also spending time with his old girlfriend who had a trailer on the outskirts of Washington, Pennsylvania.

Up until the New Year's Eve that I caught him, Jennings had successfully managed to weave his web of lies and kept us both unaware that he was spending time with each of us. As far as she knew I didn't even exist, and as for me, I had been told by Jennings that his old girlfriend had met someone else and had gotten married. His ability to lead so many different lives without tripping himself up has never ceased to astound me.

Finally, propelled by his schizophrenia, Jennings was convinced that he truly was all those things he created in his mind. Possessing the advantage of being quite handsome and dripping with charisma, his behavior was intact and not at all bizarre to those that met him. This outside reaction only fortified his convictions of his own truths about his sanity.

As pieces of information came to me over the years, one of the things I learned of Jennings' past was that as a young adult his family forced him into therapy, but he was convinced there was nothing wrong with him and refused to take his medication.

For many years his mother blamed his condition on a horseback riding incident when he was a young boy that caused him to have severe trauma to the back of his head. Later in life, as she lay on her deathbed, eaten away with cancer, she confided to me that she thought he was possessed by the Devil. Believing she lost her beloved son to the evil appetites of the demons, she lost her will to live. As his mother, she welcomed death as a release from her double-edged sword; the deterioration of her spirit because of her son's behavior and the deterioration of her body because of her cancer.

It is of no surprise that his ability to manipulate and charm his way through life continued after we were divorced and it is at this point that I lost a reality check on him. From a distance, he continued to stalk me. I would catch him sitting in his car in front of the house or leaning in a doorway across the street while I was shopping. I never knew where he would show up. I was still afraid of him, and called the police whenever he was near the house, but whatever his life was when he was not stalking me I did not care to know. The further I could separate his life from mine, the better.

On January 22, 1980, just about three years after my divorce from Jennings was final, I received a phone call from the State Police in Tionesta, Pennsylvania. Jennings was missing and was believed to have been murdered at his home in the mountains nearby. Had I seen him, they asked. No, I said, not for a few days now.

His car was in his driveway at his home in Marienville. There were no bloodstains in the soil around the property, but there were wide truck tire imprints on the ground near the house. Loose change and his keys were found scattered on the ground between the house and garage as though expelled from torn pockets in a struggle. His suitcase was still unpacked, sitting on the table where he had placed it after coming home from a visit to Pittsburgh.

I didn't cry. In my heart, the man I loved and married had died a long time ago. I could not mourn for this man. He was a stranger to me. With that single phone call, it was as though a heavy weight had been lifted from my body. I was free. Free. I was free to live and have a life again without fear. Free to walk the world again with my children without restrictions. And Jennings was finally free, released from his earthly imprisonment to go on to something more peaceful. I only hoped he didn't suffer. My thoughts flashed back to that earlier time when

Jennings proudly hovered over his dying conquest and let its blood spill onto the snow. The hunter had become the hunted.

The Pennsylvania State Police investigators kept in touch with me for a long time after Jennings' disappearance. Once they had found a body in the woods near Marion and they wanted me to send them dental records. I did. It wasn't him.

During their investigation, the detectives discovered my husband had been given a gun permit. No one had even bothered to check out his medical history. He also had been dating many women at the same time; some married; some not. And again, each thought she was the only one in his life. The poor man must have been worn out just keeping his stories straight.

The husband of one of his girlfriends allegedly had Mafia connections, and it is suspected that this husband had him targeted as retribution. But without a body they couldn't press charges. To this day, there is no death certificate. Without a certificate, there is no legal death. Without a death, there is no positive proof of crime, only conjecture.

For many years after Jennings was believed to have been murdered, I tried in vain through many channels to resolve once and for all his disappearance, but I was never able to get any circuit court judge to issue a death certificate. Having this certificate would have not only brought a certain degree of closure for us, but it would have also allowed Lee to get benefits that would have helped him through school. Jennings' murderer obviously had very strong connections in that small Pennsylvania town.

It has been over twenty years since I received that first phone call and every year since, I get a call from the Missing Persons Division of the Pennsylvania State Police, asking if I have seen Jennings; routine procedure that has to be followed.

When I now think of Jennings, I can cry. I have great compassion for the depth of pain Jennings himself must have endured. Through his eyes, in his own drama, he was the victim.

So, in the end, neither my plan, nor Jennings' plan were the ones mapped out for our lives. There was a more compelling road map charted for our journeys, and our trip ticket didn't matter. But through all of the hills and valleys in my life so far, of one thing I am certain. It is never too late to change your life for the better and shed old skin, old habits and addictions. If you have the strength to close one door behind you and open another, a better life is waiting for you on the other side; right here and right now. No matter how frightening it is to think of starting over and beginning a new journey in your life, the rewards for taking those steps forward are greater than one can imagine. I know, because I have been there and I have been given another chance to get it right this time.

In 1972 I interviewed the great violinist Rubinoff. Will Rogers had been a good friend of his and as a token of their friendship, Will gave Rubinoff a watch engraved with thoughts he shared with me.

The core thinking of what was engraved on the watch is that we go around but once in this life and we had better enjoy every minute of it while we can, because we don't have the knowledge to know when our time here is over.

Little did I dream at the time that this passing observation Rubinoff and I discussed would become an anchor to me in the hardest of times. It still today embodies much that I believe about life.

Inspired by the thoughts on Rubinoff's watch, several years ago as my children were growing up, preparing to spread their wings and fly away, I wrote the following poem that explains the essence of my life's philosophy:

Life escapes in microscopic units
Unnoticed measures of time

Silently evaporating.

A gentle surf stealing grains
As it strokes the shore of each day.

Dichotomy.

Healer. Thief.
Savior. Enemy.

Elusive, yet manageable.

The gift of Life is Time.
Use it wisely.

Ride the pendulum with wisdom,
Your dreams giving it movement.

Head clear.
Mane flowing.
Heart beating.

Inertia measuring each swing
In anticipation of its return.

Forget not one breath,
Not one tick,
Not one swing.

Forget not your purpose,
Nor your dreams.

Forget not mine.

16

When my mother died several years ago, I was left with the task of sorting though her belongings and cleaning out her house. It was during this final act of closure with the last chapter in my mother's life that I discovered an envelope she had tucked away at the back of her dresser drawer. I opened the flap that was set free by time and humidity and peeked inside. I was completely taken back by what I saw. There they were; neatly folded pages containing a handwritten diary chronicling my days with Jennings. At the time, not too sure I was ready to retrace the steps in my past life with him, I put it in my bag for later thought on the matter.

After a few days, curiosity about my mother's papers got the best of me and I sat in my favorite chair in the corner of the living room that received the warm rays of the early afternoon sun. I opened the envelope and began to leaf through its pages; the events that I had lived and had etched firmly in my mind, others that I had either forgotten or had not known about were brought back before me.

I opened the envelope to read its pages. The first page was a letter spilling with my mother's words of helplessness:

"These observations I feel I must write even though it breaks my heart to relive the nightmare we have been through since Sandra became involved with Jennings Hart. He had pursued her for six months before she would even date him. He told her that he was making much more money than he really was and he showed her this lovely home pretending that it was the home they would be moving into after they were married. Later he insisted that she sell her house so that they could move into his beautiful house. It was a lie that she realized only after her house was gone.

He was supposed to have been divorced for seven years before he met my daughter. Well into the marriage she discovered that his divorce was final only two weeks before his marriage to Sandra. We can hardly believe that this is happening to a well-educated beautiful girl and can't figure out how anyone could have such power over her. I now know how the parents feel who have children in a cult movement. We feel just helpless to control the situation. It is almost as if he has her hypnotized and she can not get out from under his spell."

I was stunned to know that my mother had been quietly grieving and living my heartache so deeply. I continued to scan the pages; picking fragments of her observations through the years:

"March 16, 1970. Sandra has been here for eight months and Jennings calls her from New Jersey two and sometimes three time a day. Usually checking to see if she comes home from her work on time. The calls come any hour of the night disturbing our sleep and keeping us constantly upset. He drives back and forth the 500 miles like it was 10. I can't believe he makes that ten-hour drive constantly. He sits up the street in his car, just to watch our house.

April 23,1970. Sandra has decided to take out an insurance policy on her life in case something happens to her and to protect her children's future. The appointment was with a family friend. When it was over and our friend left the house, Jennings started to bang on the door. He had driven all the way from New Jersey to Ohio and had been spying through the windows to look in on her. We had company this evening and everyone was here at the time. Sandra ignored the noise at the door, went to bed and we did not answer it.

May 12,1970. Today Sandra came home and said that Jennings was waiting for her at the television station and followed her again. The divorce is about to come up and Jennings is still fighting it. I think Sandra is wearing down...

July 30,1970. We can't believe it. Jennings has convinced Sandra that his attention had been only concern for her and his child and his wanting to have a second chance to make the marriage work. He told her he is going to therapy. We don't believe him. We feel helpless. I have fear of what she's walking into again. What is she thinking?

January 15,1972. We have had months of peace. It looks as though Jennings is trying to keep his word and to make their marriage whole again. I pray he does keep his word...

September 8,1974. Jennings is starting his bizarre behavior again. The doctors told Sandra that people with his condition usually get worse unless they are medicated. He is going from doctor to doctor and they tell him his symptoms are in his head.

November 23,1974. Sandra writes that Jennings is now on Lithium. It seems to be stabilizing his condition. Josh Logan was interviewed on the Today Show about this drug and how it helped him regain a normal life…

March 14,1974. We're visiting with Sandra. She is in New York today having photographs taken for an agency. Jennings is in Atlanta. He had been calling all day to check on her. I did not tell him where she was. I knew he would call her and embarrass her at the studio.

March 15,1974. Jennings met Sandra at the bus last night as she arrived to pick up her car and stepped out of the shadows in the parking lot and scared her. He had flown in from Atlanta and was waiting at the terminal for her. He had been hiding back to watch her. I called New York twice to alert her that he had come home, but she had already left.

April 29,1974. Sandra told me Jennings saw the two calls I made to New York on their phone bill and he accused her of having an affair with the photographer. He would not believe it was me who made the calls. Had he been thinking straight he would have realized that she couldn't have made the calls on that date as she already was in New York.

Page by page, I wondered at what I read, how Mother could have documented those years so accurately. I was seeing for the first time her perception of my life, as though she was with me looking over my shoulder. I read on, noticing that by this time, Mother had quit putting down dates and just wrote facts in the order they happened.

"Jennings is trying to sabotage every effort Sandra has made to get a job. He does not want her to have financial independence from him. She doesn't have much of a chance to free herself from him.

We are visiting Sandra again. The trees are in bloom but the situation here is very depressing. Jennings follows Sandra all over the house and fusses with her about everything. She went out to her car to get something and he jumped up and followed her and questioned her about her trip to the car.

My husband complained today that Jennings has been going around the house stark naked. Sandra and I were at the store and I didn't see him. It seems that it happens now every time we come to visit her.

Last night our sleep was disturbed. We saw Jennings all over the house with a flash light, looking through every cupboard, nook and cranny, even under the bed in which my husband was sleeping, looking for something. We were afraid to let him know we were awake. Sandra has to get away from him before it gets worse.

Sandra received a call today from one of her friends and we caught Jennings leaning against the corner listening to her.

I found Jennings today looking through the garbage. I don't know why. I would think that after all this time and with all of the following and checking he hasn't found Sandra doing one thing that he would give up...I think that with all the suffering ...that would be the last thing on her mind.

I received a letter from Sandra today...she is afraid of him and cannot find an escape. He does not let her out of his sight. Her situation is critical. I am losing sleep at night in fear of her safety.

Sandra writes that Jennings is now making up all sorts of stories. He claimed to have been fired from his job, but when she called his boss, he didn't know what she was talking about. He may be trying to make her feel sorry for him, but I think it is just an excuse so that he can watch her all day long. She is a prisoner and we can't help her.

One by one I turned the pages and it was as though I was reading about someone else. I was eavesdropping on a stranger's life, not mine. It was painful for me to review and relive the events in my life during those last years with Jennings.

As I read on, I became brutally aware that this woman I was reading about didn't seem to be me. I didn't know who this person was. Why didn't she get out of this destructive relationship earlier? Why did she stay in there so long without trying to flee? Why didn't she realize that there was no hope for his getting well and that the longer she stayed the more destructive it was for both her and her children?

Reading the final pages of my mother's diary, I saw a woman, who for good reason, was so completely frightened of her husband, she became emotionally paralyzed. It sickened me to be able to face for the first time, the person I used to be and how I got there. I could not understand why I was willing to tolerate and accept dysfunction as normalcy.

I've always been a 'fixer'. The one who always tries to make things right; whole. In my work, I am a perfectionist. I take pleasure achieving, working out problems, solving and creating successful solutions. That may be commended in the business world, but in one's personal life it doesn't always work. As the doctor told me earlier, there is a point to stop beating you head against the wall.

After reading Mother's diary, for the first time I was forced to face who I was then; a person who put blinders on and tried to be strong, when, most definitely, I should have run. But in my defense, I do remember feeling both afraid and trapped. The police couldn't help me until Jennings took violent action against me. At the time, there were no hostels like there are today. As a victim of spousal abuse, I was in a powerful emotional cyclone that completely enveloped me. I guess it all came down to my reasoning that no matter what, he would have found me anyway. To this day, I'm still sure of that. Just as he did when he pursued his four legged creatures, he would not have allowed me to get away again. Jennings would have hunted me down to the end. My fate was in the hands of God's divine plan for me and although I took precautions to be aware of Jennings' presence while following me, there was nothing I could do about it.

According to Blakeston New Gould Dictionary (McGraw-Hill) schizophrenia is now classified as a schizophrenic reaction. Schizophrenic reaction is one group of psychotic reactions often beginning after adolescence or in young adulthood. These reactions are characterized by fundamental disturbances in reality, relationships and concept formations. As in Jennings' case also, these are accompanied by the associated affective behavior; as well as intellectual disturbances to varying degrees and mixtures.

These reactions can be marked by a tendency to withdraw from reality or appropriate mood. Those afflicted often display unpredictable disturbances in the stream of thought, regressive tendencies to the point of deterioration. The acute stages of schizophrenia reaction are often accompanied by hallucinations and delusions.

There are several types of schizophrenia; catatonic, or those that remain in a stupor; childhood type; psychotic reaction in young children; and those that suffer from paranoia.

Jennings suffered from the last type. Paranoid schizophrenia is a form in which delusions of persecution or of grandeur, or both, predominate and sometimes are systemized. As with my husband, the patient is often more intact and less bizarre in other areas, but generally hostile and sometimes hypochrondriachal.

It was Jennings' ability to appear normal to all around him that allowed his disease to go unchecked for so many years. And because of this information that I know about schizophrenia, I am not so hard on myself now for not suspecting his behavior. It was only when Jennings' schizophrenia developed into the acute stages, did he trip himself up. By that time, his illness was out of control and so was his behavior. And it eventually cost him his life.

In 1995, as part of a healing process for me concerning my life with Jennings was to release my repressed feelings about my late husband. As a journalist and actress, the best outlet for me was to put my thoughts on paper. The resulting work was a ninety-minute one-woman narrative that, in turn, spawned the birth of this memoir.

Initially, I wrote *Behind The Magic Mirror* as a creative catharsis; as an emotional healing. Then last summer while I was cleaning out the attic in preparation for my first garage sale, I came across a box of old tapes my son had recorded before he left for Los Angeles about eight years ago.

As I played the music and listened intently to the lyrics of each song, I could hear his pain. He, too, was reaching out for unresolved answers. I realized then, more than ever, I was not alone in my quest for closure and my work for closure was not finished.

It was at that moment that I knew the story did not end with the phone call from the state police in 1980, it ends when we know what happened to Jennings during his last days in Marienville. The following day I started my search for the truth about Jennings and what really happened to him. I unlocked the desk drawer where I had put Mother's diary and opened the next phase of Jennings' story.

I began a final investigative journey that took me to Marienville where I unlocked the mystery of Jennings' disappearance. The result of the next phase, the last chapters of Jennings' life is the true-crime story as it unfolded before me.

Death Certificate

PART 2

17

On January 21, 1980, my fifty-year old ex-husband disappeared. He was six feet tall and weighed 180 pounds. He had black and gray hair, a beard and mustache. He was reported to be last seen that afternoon around 3 p.m. wearing a windbreaker and dark jeans.

Jennings was missing and suspected to have met with foul play. Murder, he said. I felt a freedom I had never experienced in years. I was finally free. Free to live. Free to have a life again. The tears that did not come that day were for happiness, not for sorrow. I could not mourn for this man. The man that I had loved and married, the Jennings that I had known, died a long time ago. I only hoped that he hadn't suffered.

If I thought the call from the Pennsylvania State Police that cold January morning in 1980 was a call of freedom, emancipating me from the bonds of terror I had experienced at the hands of my ex-husband, the release from emotional captivity was short lived.

Every day of every year since that fateful call, my children and I have lived without closure. Day in and day out we have lived our lives, on the surface happy and productive, but lying beneath in each of us has been the emptiness of not knowing.

It was years before I could even talk about my life with Jennings. I had buried my pain safely, deep within in a part of me and I was not ready to share it with anyone, even my children.

It was only after my son started releasing his grief through his music as a songwriter that I realized the only way we could have complete closure in our chapters with Jennings was to find out what really happened to him. There had always been strong conjecture that he had been murdered, but it was always just that. They had never been able to find his body, but the assumption on all levels of authority was that he was no longer alive.

I knew that if I were going to try to discover the truth about Jennings' disappearance, I would have to begin honing my investigative reporter skills that I had not used in many years. I had to approach this case with an open mind and examine the facts about the supposed victim with objectivity.

What are the basic facts? I had to look at the facts as I knew them. At least it was a start. Where to begin my search for Jennings, the real Jennings Hart? Who was he and just how was I to begin to find the pieces, his raison d'être, that would lead me to the answers that would help me tell you his story?

What I know about his life before I met him is easy to tell. As a young man he was drafted into the Korean Conflict, stationed in Germany and proudly served his time singing with the Army Band and the USO. His clear tenor voice had echoed throughout the vaulted chapels in many of the grand cathedrals in Europe, his tour of duty exposing him to wonders beyond his simple childhood life on his parent's farm.

But these regal foreign cities and bucolic countryside; young apple-cheeked Frauleins tempting him with their smiles and other things more lusting could not keep him from dreaming for the day when he could go home.

Uncle Sam may have taken the boy away from the farm, but the farm stayed within the boy and at the end of his tour, he was more than anxious to return home to the comforting hills of Washington, Pennsylvania. He married his local sweetheart and thus in doing so, buried his youthful dreams of singing his way to riches deep within his blue collar existence, and even further still into his subconscious.

Life went along smoothly for him for awhile. He and his young wife had three children. He had a good job as a mould maker in a local glass plant and was leading a comfortable life, or at least it appeared so on the surface. But quietly underneath this facade, dark conflicts were beginning to simmer inside of him.

It was at this time that his inner demons began to manifest themselves and consume his being. Those who were close to him noticed a fundamental disturbance in reality of his thoughts and were reluctant witnesses to the budding of his bizarre behavior.

In time, he began finding solace in the arms of other women and weaving for them a web of lies about who he was. He created for himself many personalities, perhaps some of which contained unfulfilled dreams and achievements he felt the world denied him.

The truth is that Jennings believed all those things he created in his mind, and to his advantage, for those who were not close to him, his behavior was intact and not at all bizarre. He was dripping with good looks and charisma, a lethal combination for deceit.

He created different scenarios to tell each of his women. He was the rough macho man for the sexy bar fly. He was the sophisticated and successful businessman for the upscale women that he attracted. He would attend the ballet, then just as easily shift gears and hang in seedy bars to romance a woman over a few beers.

Finally, after years of enduring his infidelities, his fed-up wife separated from him, and his family also having had enough of his shenanigans, forced him into therapy. Even though he remained convinced there was nothing wrong with him, he attended the perfunctory sessions to keep everyone happy.

His mother blamed his condition on a horseback riding accident that caused trauma to the back of his head when he was a child. Years later, when I was her daughter-in-law, as she lay on her deathbed, dying of cancer, she confided to me that she was totally convinced that he was possessed by the Devil. Believing she lost her beloved son to the evil appetites of the demons, she lost her will to fight the ills that were eating away at her earthly flesh. She welcomed death as a release from her double-edged sword.

Jennings' mother, how could I ever forget her? The last time I saw her before her death, I had come to visit in her modest ranch house in Washington, Pennsylvania. She was in bed, weakened by her illness. Her once strong frame appeared frail under the light sheet that covered her body and exposed the outline of her thin form. She motioned for me to come close to her bed so that she could speak to me without strain. We talked about her son and her lost hopes for her favored child. We both were suffering in our own way in dealing with Jennings. She stretched out her arm toward me and reached for me, her frail hand lined with blue rivers of life, their rounded swells seemingly floating on the surface of her translucent skin.

I expected her hand to be cold, but it was warm and soft as she held mine. She then turned my hand, and placing and object there, gently folded my fingers to encase it securely. "I should have given this to you a long time ago. I'm sorry."

She then indicated she was tired, so I bent and kissed her on her forehead and walked out of the room. I sensed that it might be the last time I would see her alive, and that in her way, she was saying goodbye.

As I walked through the living room to the kitchen where we had spent so many happy times, and curious about her gift to me, I opened my hand to see what she had placed there. In the cup of my palm was a small gold heart pin.

As I had feared, Elizabeth closed her eyes and said goodbye to her sorrows for the final time, making me the sole benefactor of her concerns for her son. Her troubles in this life were over, but unfortunately for my future, not telling me, not revealing the well-kept secret that could have saved me; that her son was other than I thought her was, affected my future greatly. The gift, her most precious material possession, I was soon to realize was her way of payment to her daughter-in-law for my pain. I had inherited her burden because I was married to her son.

Her gold heart now rests inside a small red velvet box in the top drawer of my dresser, waiting to be passed on to another. It was only when I watched my third child, my only son, grow into manhood, that I appreciated the unique bond between mother and son, and I now understand her loyalty to Jennings and her reluctance to expose her son's demons. Yet, in retrospect, I am left with the reality that even she, Jennings' own mother, did not really know him. She did not want to recognize his mental illness and blamed it all on the Devil inside of him. She thought that I would be the savior that would exorcise the Evil.

And so these are the truths about Jennings; where he came from and how he lived, and how he was loved by many that knew him well, but in reality, knew him not.

In telling my story, I relied on my mother's recollections from her diary. These helped stimulate forgotten memories of my own about my husband. I realize that Jennings' presence, in my mind, and on these pages, now seems only to weave in and out of my life as though a ghost. The true essence of who he was I cannot conjure; a true human character for you to grasp to help you understand who this man was that I loved, and after much deliberation, I have come to the truth as I see it.

To this day, it is as though he is still a mere shadow or semblance; a vague apparition that still haunts me. He was not one, but a chameleon, a kaleidoscope of beings in one form and I did not then, nor do I now really know who he was; this truth impeding the passage of words that would convey his persona and the reasons I brought this man into my life.

During the period in my writing that I was struggling with my emotions, trying to put the chapters in my life with Jennings on paper, I took an evening off to see the edgy comedic movie starring Cameron Diaz and Ben Stiller, *"There's Something About Mary."*

Deeply immersed in my own story and unable to detach my mind from my work, even while away from my computer, I watched the film. I suddenly became aware I was witnessing the special 'something' of Cameron's Mary; her beauty that appealed to the male senses; her honesty and her ability to look beneath the surface and transcend the limitations of the physical form; her willingness to see an inner worth that others often missed.

Thinking about that film somehow opened a liberating avenue of thought about the decisions in my life I made about Jennings after he so blatantly violated my trust in him, time and time again. Jennings had a 'something', not like Mary's 'something', but his own unique 'something'.

He had good looks and unbelievable charm that short-circuited one's ability to see who he really was, and thus enabled him to convince his most intelligent and sophisticated friends that he was someone he wasn't. But unlike Mary, he used his 'something' for selfish reasons. Very few, if any, were able to see beyond that 'something' that Jennings projected. I was not alone.

He was a master at his craft, propelled by his schizophrenia. And when he held his hand out to me, I stepped into his web, mesmerized by his persona, unable to resist his persistent declarations of undying love for me. He slowly began to wrap me in the strong threads of mental imprisonment until I was weakened beyond escape and primed for his deadly poisonous strike.

His focus was so clear and it was as though I really had no choice once he had set his sights on me. I had to be a part of his life forever. As long as I was alive, as long as he was alive, I was destined to be imprisoned by his obsession with me.

Personally, knowing what I knew about him, it would be of no surprise to me if Jennings used his ability to manipulate and charm his way through life after we were divorced. It is at that point that I lost a reality check on him, even though I was still stalked by Jennings and I was afraid of him. But whatever his life was when he was not stalking me, I had not cared to know.

The further I could separate his life from mine, the better. Now I was faced with the difficult task of filling in the blank pages of Jennings' life after he left the hospital and returned to Pennsylvania.

The first piece of the puzzle was to send for Jennings' hospital records so that I could see firsthand what was going on in his mind according to the physicians at the hospital. I was certain that his medical history was incarcerated somewhere deep within the bowels of the hospital's medical archives.

Just how soon they would be retrieved was another question. My need, my anticipation, was much more urgent, and the receipt of the documents might not be as timely as I would like, but it was the most logical beginning point for me.

Not knowing whether I really was ready to fill my head with additional information about Jennings, I was propelled forward now by a growing curiosity not only about Jennings, but also about myself; the woman I was in his schizophrenic eyes.

I called Riverview Hospital and sent my request for his records in writing. Two weeks later the envelope containing the information I had requested arrived. I carefully unsealed the envelope, confident as to what I would discover. I wasn't disappointed. The pages read as I had expected.

My eyes scanned the first page. Age: 46. I hadn't remembered he was so young.

'Notify in case of emergency… wife, Sandra.

Birth place. Ohio.'

Ah, there it was, 'Schizophrenia.' That was the fist time I had actually seen documentation of his admitting diagnosis.

I moved on to the next page. 'Final Diagnosis: Schizophrenic reaction, paranoid type.' And then there followed the physician's observation of his illness.

"Patient seemed highly suspicious and shortly after being on the floor expressed resentment about hospitalization. The patient had been acting bizarrely and had been quite suspicious that his wife was unfaithful to him. He is delusional. Patient has had history of hospitalization prior to this for similar symptoms. At the time of my examination, he was oriented to all spheres. His answers to questions were time guarded. He seemed to be highly suspicious and this was directed mostly towards his wife and also towards his fellow employees. The patient was heading for delusion but denies any type of hallucinations." Again the doctor's signature appeared at the bottom of the page.

Ironically, I noted also the information I had just read was dictated on my birthday of that year, and little was I to suspect four years later that would also be the month he disappeared forever.

On the third page of the report what I read I remembered well, what was noted on the report; that first telephone message from the hospital telling me my husband had escaped and was probably on his way back home. He was picked up by the police and convinced to readmit himself. ‘This patient one day after his admission AMA. He had left the ward and had not returned.” Again the doctor’s signature was below this information.

The final time Jennings was again admitted to the hospital was after he had attacked me in our bedroom and I was able to escape and call the police. This time the diagnosis read, “Acute schizophrenia.” He had progressed that deeply into his illness.

As I read on, page by page, it suggested the profile of a very disturbed man who allowed the doctors very little insight into who he really was.

During his final hospital stay his affect and moods did improve with medication and supportive therapy. Upon his discharge he was told to continue with this treatment and medication as an outpatient.

He, through his psychotic genius, behaved and told them what they wanted to hear until he was able to free himself. And once he had that freedom, he did what he pleased with no medication and no therapy. Jennings knew so well how to manipulate his doctors.

He was a walking time bomb. Under these conditions the odds were stacked against him. Sooner or later he had to self-destruct. It was only a matter of time

I tried hard to remember the name of the town Jennings moved to when he started working again. I thought it could be Marion. That was the name of the glass plant where he worked. I thought I remembered seeing the name on the envelopes when Jennings would send letters to us.

I called information and got the number of the state police barracks that would have been responsible for that territory. After sixteen years the only name I could remember was the first name of the detective I had spoken to so often.

I didn't know anything else about Marion, only that it was a very small town on the edge of the Allegheny Mountains and at least a seven -hour drive from where I lived in New Jersey.

From my initial conversations in 1980 with the detectives on the case I knew there had been coverage of Jennings' disappearance in the local newspapers at the time. I got out our road atlas and scanned the Pennsylvania map for Marion and surrounding larger towns that may have reported the incident in their newspaper. I couldn't find any town called Marion on the map.

I called information. "Sorry. No Marion." The operator said.

"Are you sure?" I questioned. "Or something close to that?"

There was silence.

"Marion or something close to that?" I repeated myself.

He came back on the line. "Could it be Marienville?" he offered.

"Yes. Yes. That's it." I remembered. It was Marienville. "Do you have a listing for a Marienville newspaper?"

"No.

"Library?"

"No." he replied.

I was frustrated and quickly looked at the Atlas again to find Marienville, or a bigger dot near Marienville. I found one. Oil City.

"Oil City?" I crossed my fingers.

"Newspaper or library?" he questioned.

"Newspaper, no both, library, too." While I had him I was going to get both sources if I needed them.

The first number I tried was the newspaper's, the Oil City Derrick. No one picked up the phone. I looked at my watch and it was seven o'clock. Maybe it's a weekly and there is no night shift around.

Next I tried the library and I connected. A young woman answered. I asked her if the library kept microfilms of stories from the local newspapers and explained to her why I asked. She confirmed that they did indeed have such records and that with specific dates she would access those files to see if she could find anything.

I hoped that the records would bring us something that would at least get me started in the right direction and enable me to start compiling facts about Jennings' disappearance. I also asked her what state police unit would be responsible for the Marienville area. She said she wasn't sure, but probably the Tionesta one. I gave her my address and telephone number and thanked her for her help.

It took only a week for the information to arrive. She was true to her word and I got lucky. She had found several articles, not only in the Oil City Derrick, but the Clarion News as well. The articles spanned a period of three years, beginning several days after his disappearance and then annually for the next two years.

I eagerly devoured the articles headlined. "Description Given For Missing Man", "Father Missing", "Man disappeared 1 Year Ago today", "Man Missing For Three Years". There they were. All that was left of my husband were headlines reaching out for answers.

People caring for three years, then nothing. The press gave up. His family gave up, at least their public appeals. Jennings was forgotten by most, but not all. The one lone person who never gave up and worked the hardest to solve the mystery was the state police investigator assigned to the case from day one. Until his retirement, he never gave up hope of finding the answers.

My investigation was beginning at the end. On January 21, 1980, Jennings disappeared. He reportedly returned home from Pittsburgh that morning, where he had been visiting with family members. His car and home were found unlocked and his keys and wallet were found in his house.

Reports are that he left his work about an hour early where he was a supervisor at Glass Containers Corporation in Marienville. He had stopped to buy gas before driving the eight miles south to his home.

The newspaper articles chronicle that he had plans to meet a friend later and when he did not show up she started looking for him and eventually called the police.

Jennings' family filed a missing person report after not being able to contact him for awhile. The state police investigated and found that nothing was missing from the house and there was no trace of him. The police said it was as though he went for a walk and never returned.

My thoughts were that more than likely, he was erased. I knew my husband too well and I knew he would not just go away. He wouldn't let go of me. He wouldn't leave, I knew him well enough to know.

It was becoming increasingly clear to me that if I was really going to delve deeply into my husband's life during those final days in Marienville, I couldn't do it over the phone.

The place I had blocked out of my mind for so many years and that represented bondage would now represent a pilgrimage to my freedom. I would go, but I didn't want to go alone. My husband, Arthur, whom I married in 1985, would join me. Jennings and his mysterious disappearance had always been an eternal shadow in my present life and marriage, so it was a journey we felt we should take together.

Although the children had grown up and found their own lives, they also were still coping with our past. My son, at twenty-six had a great curiosity about life that was still ripe, but there was a deeper edge to him for a man so young. He had found his life in his own way. From the pieces of his broken childhood he had found a reason for being. He had discovered the glue that would hold him together and make him deal with his closure, his music. I was still fighting to find my way. I was hoping this trip and my efforts to find the truth about Jennings would help us find some degree of peace.

I was still struggling with not only my past, but also dealing with the future and the loss of time for my own dreams because of the years Jennings stole from me. But through my son's example of getting on with his life, he now had become the teacher and I the pupil.

My daughters, Brett and Alison, too, seemed on the surface to have found their acceptance of the past. The only thing that we all still had unresolved was our passion for knowledge as to what happened to Jennings.

18

Arthur and I rose at dawn to get an early start. We wanted to be on our way and onto Route 80 before the traffic in the urban areas would clog this major western artery that would carry us to Marienville, Pennsylvania.

We were going to travel the road that Jennings had driven so many times spurred by his obsessive paranoia and bizarre need to monitor my life in New Jersey after our divorce.

A strange twist of fate it was indeed that would place Arthur and I on this same route now in search of Jennings and his life after our divorce.

It was a beautiful spring morning and as we rode along I glanced over at my husband, his strong handsome profile silhouetted against the light of the passing landscape. So much time has passed for us, I thought. My eyes followed the outline of his white wavy hair and I thought of how good he had been to my children, and now how supportive of me on this journey that really wasn't even his.

We were riding, listening to my son's music on the tape deck, the poetic and soulful lyrics echoing his pain and wonder at life. I could feel the influence that his father's disappearance had on him. We all knew how devastating the twin burdens of schizophrenia and an unsolved mystery can be on a family. It cripples and changes explorations and expectations in life. He might not have become such a powerful lyricist and may not have turned to music as a catharsis for his suffering had his life been otherwise.

It is as if by exorcising memories of his father through his music he can finally understand him. Unlike his father he was going to make his life count. He was willing to work hard for his dreams and he wasn't going to pass through this life only taking. I hope it happens for him, I hope he receives back as much as he gives.

The closer we got to Maryville the more I realized why Jennings chose to come to this area. The surrounding countryside was very much like where he grew up. The roads were dotted on each side with farms and acres of plowed fields. The foreground was flat and rolled along to meet the foothills of the mountains in the distance and the trees were still in dark gray and brown winter dress. Everything seemed so, still, so peaceful. This was his place, I thought. This was where he felt safe and comfortable. This was the real Jennings.

We turned off route 80 and took a winding country road that would take us north to our destination. As we turned off, on my left I saw a horse and buggy going down a small side road.

"There must be an Amish community around here," I said turning to Arthur.

"Probably. Don't these ranch houses remind you of the ones in Western Pennsylvania? It's just like there, isn't it? Kind of spooky don't you think, since that is where Jennings grew up?" I said.

"Yes. Like he found a home away from home."

We passed more houses and trailers, each with a pickup truck or some other form of four-wheel drive vehicle in the yard or driveway. If it wasn't a four-wheeler it was an old model of something a bit rusty and longer than my living room and definitely wasn't foreign built.

"That sign said eleven miles to Marienville, we're almost there," Arthur said. "This must be a big hunting and camping area. Look at all the cabins. Jennings really must have been in heaven out here," he indicated pointing to our right.

I glanced out my window at the wooded landscape that looked so desolate except for a scattering of boarded up cabin encampments. As I looked beyond the edge of the road and into the horizon, the only signs of life I could see were slim ribbons of smoke here and there rising from the darkness deep within the heart of the mountains. I felt a tinge of loneliness just witnessing the isolation.

The movement of the car along the winding road past the rows of tall and narrow trees in the sunset flashed the light across our eyes in a hypnotizing flicker simulating the light rhythms of a silent movie. It made the passing scenery take on an almost surreal appearance.

My trance was broken by my husband's voice, "Hey, a 'Chad and Dad's' sign there above that store. Boy, are we in the boonies," he said in his worst mountain mimic.

"Very funny, but I bet you can find everything you would want in there, from beer to clothes pins."

"No doubt," he said. "Looks like they do a lot of logging here, too. Look at the piles of logs over there and the old tracks behind them. Maybe they used to carry them by train somewhere to a mill. I hate to see the forests stripped. They are so beautiful here."

He was right. The area did look desolate with just a few trees standing alone among the stacked logs. My thoughts went back to Jennings and his love for hunting and how circumstances had been reversed. He, instead of his prey, had been cut down in the prime of his life, leaving a great emptiness against the sky.

As we drove on we passed the Crown General Store with its sign announcing 'Corn For Critters And Fresh Produce For Humans'. Well, that's creative, I thought. Next came the town's little white post office and a sporting goods store. The latter fortifying our thought that this must be a big hunting area. Maybe even for fishing in the streams that were now flush with fresh water rolling down from the mountain. We had had a record snow fall in the East during winter and all of the rivers and streams were filled to capacity with melted snow from the mountain tops that sometimes threatened to escape beyond the lips of the waterways. This area must be very beautiful in the summer when the rivers and lakes are filled and the mountains become green again, I thought.

"This must be the edge of town, there is the Pigeon Loft Hotel. Signs of life are near, I hope." Arthur said removing his sunglasses. The sun was beginning to set and we were just on the verge of losing the day to twilight.

"Gunsmoke?" Arthur started to laugh.

"What are you laughing about?"

"That house back there. They had a big sign on it by the door; 'Gunsmoke'.

"So what else is new?" I said. "We personalize our license plates with tags as 'EGO' and 'SUCCESS' and our initials. And back at the shore everyone who has over an acre christens their property with names like Seven Chimneys or Fore Views, why not Gunsmoke on that homestead? Guess that proves we are not as far from civilization after all! Besides, we name our dogs, don't we? Why not our houses? It gives us a sense of owning something. Being a capitalist, even on a small level feels good. It's the American way."

"Okay, if you say so. I still think it's kind of strange." Leave it to Arthur to always have the last word.

The sun was just about retired for the day as we pulled in to the Old Bucktail Motel where a Vacancy sign was hung in full view of the road on the edge of the main street in town. There wasn't enough light left for a picture, so we checked in and decided we would drive up into town and find some place to eat.

We drove the short distance into Mairenville and it looked like any other small mountain town with its narrow main street and shops unevenly scattered along the edges of the road. We passed the Village Diner and turned right across old railroad tracks to the Kelly Hotel and Restaurant. We found a parallel parking spot next to a red pickup in front of the Shamrock Dining Room that was part of the hotel. The Kelly Hotel was two-story red brick building with a western style porch and a sloped roof that ran the length of the building. The side of the building facing the main street was painted white with "KELLY HOTEL" printed in large green letters.

It was St. Patrick's Day and we decided this would be an appropriate place to have our first meal. Over a big plate of corned beef and cabbage that tasted like it came directly out of my grandma's kitchen, we talked about how we could maximize our time there and how we could open up information to us without drawing too much attention to ourselves. I personally was a little nervous about asking too many questions, in case we were opening up old wounds among townsfolk who probably knew more than we did.

First, I wanted to find Jennings' house. The State Police could give us additional information about his disappearance. Tomorrow that should be our first stop, the Tionesta barracks. Maybe an officer who was around when Jennings first disappeared could help shed some light on the case.

After dinner we walked out into the crisp mountain air and Arthur stretched his arms and took a long deep breath.

"Feels good, doesn't it?' I said following his lead. "The air here smells so clean."

"Bet it brings back a lot of memories, doesn't it, Sandra?"

I silently nodded in thinking of my first days with Jennings in Pennsylvania and suddenly felt very tired.

"Tomorrow's going to be a big day," Arthur said looking up at the clear night sky. "Let's go back to the Bucktail and turn in."

Sounded good to me.

19

The next morning we arose early and headed ten miles north to the Tionesta State Police Barracks. It was easy to find but the trail led to a dead end. The trooper I had spoken with years ago had retired from the force and when I called his house his answering machine was taking messages. He had gone to Florida for the winter.

I inquired as to whom else I could speak with there that might know about the case. That trooper wasn't there either and wouldn't be back until Tuesday. A call by the dispatcher to his house found him out of town, also. The dispatcher was alone and all of the troopers were in their cars patrolling the county.

"Let's go back to town," Arthur suggested.

"Good idea. Someone must still be around who remembers Jennings."

Our first stop was the Bucktail Hotel across from the Kelly Hotel.

I walked into the bar where the barmaid was busily chatting with her two lone customers at the far end of the bar. She was an attractive blond, I would guess in her early fifties.

"Is that building down this road the old glass factory?" I thought that would be good for openers.

"Yea," she answered with a slight twang. "It's really run down now though. It closed up years ago."

Well, here goes I thought, "How long have you lived here?"

She looked at me and didn't answer right away. "About sixteen years," she finally replied. "Why you askin'?"

"Do you remember a man by the name of Jennings Hart. He used to work at the glass factory."

"Yea. Isn't he the guy that disappeared?"

"That's right. Do you know where he lived, where his house would be?"

"No. But if you go across the street to the Kelly Hotel there, in the bar, ask for a guy, Joe. He works with the ambulances and stuff. He was there."

"Oh great, thanks a lot."

I practically bounded down the few steps to the parking lot where Arthur had been busily taking pictures.

"There is a man called Joe who runs the Kelly Hotel or bar or something. The woman inside the Bucktail said he was there and would know where Jennings lived. Let's go."

We entered the hotel through the same entrance we used the night before and the waitress directed us right through the doors to the bar area. As we opened the door a sea of darkness and smoke met us. I don't think there was a window in the place, and all I could see at first, were neon beer signs fogged over by the patrons' Winstons.

Our eyes soon adjusted to the darkness and I approached the barmaid, the nearest person to me.

"Is Joe here?

"No."

"Where can I find him?"

"He's in North Carolina."

Well, two strikes, but I still wasn't out. I wasn't going to quit now. Someone in this place had to know where Jennings lived. "Is there anyone here who has lived here for along time, maybe over sixteen years?" I asked.

She turned away from me and looked toward the bar area. She moved her head back and forth slowly along the bar then pointed to the far center of the large oak horseshoe that was packed with customers. I couldn't tell which man she meant.

Seeing my disorientation she motioned for Arthur and I to follow her and she pointed again at a man hunched over his drink at the far end of the bar.

I thanked her and we walked down the far side of the bar and stopped behind the man. He was wearing a dark windbreaker and an stained red ball cap pushed back to allow clearance for the hoisting of a brew or two.

"Hi. Don't mean to bother you, but the woman behind the bar there thought you might know a man by the name of Jennings Hart who disappeared from here about sixteen years ago." This time it was Arthur asking the questions. He was hoping the man would turn around.

The dark windbreaker and the old ball cap swiveled on his bar seat and looked up at us. My guess is that he was in his seventies and had seen a lot of outdoors in his time. The lines in his face were defined, etched from years of abuse and the natural ravages of age. He smiled as he slid off his seat to face us and leaned one arm on the back of his chair.

His greeting revealed that he had several teeth missing in prominent places. "Yuh. Was supervisor at the plant here," he said slowly. He vigorously rubbed his eyes before he spoke. Either he had something preoccupying his mind or the heavy smoke in the room was bothering him. I really didn't care. For our purposes all we wanted were answers.

"Let's see, do you know where 899 is..." He was drunk, but we waited patiently for him to organize this thoughts, hoping to get the directions to Jennings' house.

“ ’Bout eight miles down the road," he continued slowly, "on the right…a red brick cottage…has a Virgin Mary in the yard. Do you know where that is?”

Arthur and I both shook our heads, indicating that we didn't have a clue. Now it was getting laborious.

“…Eight miles straight down the road until you come to a red brick cottage…”

“I think we can find it," I said trying to hurry him along, “and from there, what?”

He rubbed his eyes again. This was worse than pulling teeth.

“Well, you turn there, left. You know where 899 is…?”

“We’ll find it,” Arthur said motioning for the barmaid to come over. “I’d like to by him a drink,” he said handing her a couple of dollars.

The old man smiled and ordered another beer.

As we thanked him and turned to leave, he pulled at my sleeve, “Can I ask you something?”

“Sure, what is it?” I responded, genuinely wondering what could be on his mind.

“Was he in the Mafia?”

His question took me by surprise. “Did you hear that he was?”

“Folks here about thought.”

Before he could finish, I stepped in. “No,” I replied, “he wasn’t.” I hoped that I was telling the truth.

Arthur and I opened the door and walked out of that abyss into the crisp spring air and welcomed the light of day. But a new avenue of thought had been opened up by the red ball cap and dark windbreaker we left back in the bar with his beer. We didn’t speak until we reached the car.

“What do you think?" I asked him.

“Maybe we just found the key to open this can of worms, but first, let’s see if we can find his house.”

A chill went through me and I started to get a little nervous. In a small town like this the odds are that someone was in Kelly's bar that St. Patrick's Day that knew more about what happened to Jennings than the old man. If they weren't directly within earshot, conversations could travel quickly along the large horseshoe shaped bar to ears interested in what business we strangers had with the old man.

Arthur reminded me that I had always had an active imagination and that I could start a panic in a monastery. But I know my husband and I knew that he had real concerns, also, that I just may be right.

We were silent, immersed in our own thoughts until we spotted the small brick house on my side of the road. I saw a large Virgin Mary statue in the front yard.

"This must be it, turn right here."

Arthur turned the car left and traveled down slowly about 300 feet and there it was sitting back off the road in a clearing edged by a row of tall thin trees. Surrounding the clearing on each side were thick woods.

It was not at all what I expected. All of these years I pictured the house entirely set in deep woods and not visible from the road. I envisioned it more to be a large cabin other than the house that I saw.

In reality, the house was a square structure about 25 feet across and painted brick red with one small high window next to a front door in the center of the house. The roof was gently peaked and the eve area was painted white, forming a triangle ending just above the top of the door.

In the center of the roof was a lookout tower. Lee had told me earlier that he remembered his dad writing and saying it had been a forest ranger station at one time. That would explain the tower.

There was an old shed to the left of the house and a two-car garage about 40 feet away and a pile of wood near the right side. We could see smoke curling low from both the house chimney and what looked like a curing shed near the woodpile.

The winding dirt driveway had along both edges and placed every ten feet or so twenty gallon white plastic pails, probably filled with sand for icy trips on the driveway. And smack dab in the middle of it all was a high wood utility pole.

So finally, there it was. The place Jennings escaped to after our divorce and the place where possibly he drew his last breath.

Arthur parked the car on the edge of the road and we stood there, our arms around one another. Together we had embarked upon a journey committed to the end, whatever it may be. He took a few pictures and we went back up the pitted road that lead us back to 899 and our motel.

20

Again I was up with the sun the next morning. The clear mountain air seemed to be giving me a charge of energy I hadn't experience in a long time. I roused Arthur out of a deep sleep just after sunrise and lured him from our room with the promise of fresh pancakes and eggs at the Kelly Inn in exchange for an early start to our day.

The night before we both had decided that we would go back to town and snoop around a bit more, but in Arthur's mind I'm sure he did not have my same urgency and early deadlines.

I sat on the stoop of the long porch of the motel and buttoned my jacket against the morning chill. It was so quiet I could hear the silence. Now and then the stillness was interrupted by the sounds of chirping birds in the tall trees above me, but that was all.

No traffic or boom boxes, just wonderful silence met my ears. I tried to think of the phrase my grandfather always used to tell us grandchildren when we would interrupt his concentration during church services. Something about silence is golden. The quiet reminded me of that dear old man and my happy childhood days spent on his farm.

I remember sitting early in the morning at the big picnic table under the tall pine trees in their front yard. The table had attached benches and was splintered and weathered to a silvery gray color. I would sit there in my pajamas, my short legs hanging from the bench, my feet just far enough to reach the top of the moist uncut grass beneath it. I would swing my legs back and forth, back and forth to feel the cool dampness of the dewy green spikes slide across my feet. I would sit there dreaming and listening to the silence and waiting for the world to awake.

I heard the door open behind me. "What time is it, anyway?" The birds aren't even awake! What's got into you?"

I turned and saw Arthur poking his gray morning mop of a head out of the doorway.

"Oh, I don't know. Too much oxygen in this air and I couldn't sleep. Come on, it's after six already. Get dressed and we'll drive into town and get a hot breakfast. We have a lot to do today. We've got to find someone with answers and we might as well make the most of our day. Okay?"

"Jees it's cold," he said as he turned back into his room, "at least let me brush my teeth." Spoken just like a boy from the Bronx, I thought, as I heard the door slam behind him to keep out the cold.

By six-thirty we were headed for town and the start of our day. Not surprisingly the tables were already filled with locals loading up on sausages and eggs, black coffee and the second round of nicotine to start their motors.

"See," I said to my husband, "'your wife is not so crazy after all. Five minutes later and we wouldn't have gotten a seat."

Arthur put his arm around my shoulder, "Okay, Mom. Right again as usual. Let's grab that booth over there." He pointed to one next to the back of the room. "I wouldn't be surprised if Jennings came here a lot, it's so close to the plant. Maybe one of the waitresses would remember him, do you think?"

"Maybe. It wouldn't hurt to ask."

He picked up his menu. I noticed that it had stains of other meals past on the outside cover facing me.

"Any oatmeal listed in there?" I asked. "I just want coffee and maybe a muffin."

"What kind of muffin?"

"Oh, I don't care. Bran?"

"Today's your lucky day. Oatmeal and muffins are right here."

"What are you having?" knowing the answer before I asked.

"Pancakes and eggs look good, with a side of home fries."

"Have you had your cholesterol checked lately?"

"Who cares. Let's think of this as a vacation and anything goes on vacation, right?"

Youth, I thought. Where did it go and why so fast? I would just be happy with my oatmeal and thank God I can still touch my toes without bending my knees. But I wasn't as risky as my husband in the food department.

There only seemed to be two waitresses in the place, and one that came to our table seemed a little too young to have been at her job in Jennings' day, but we asked anyway. She said no, but volunteered to ask the other waitress if she knew Jennings.

I was sitting and soulfully watching my husband polish off the last bite of his syrup-laden homemade pancakes when the older waitress approached our table.

"Y'all the folks askin' about that guy that disappeared some years back?" she said with a heavy southern drawl.

I was taken back by her accent. What would a southern girl be doing here? I imagined that she came to this area with a husband or lover. Although whatever her reason for being in Marienville at any other time would have captured my curiosity, now my only interest was if she could help us in our search.

"Yes. Jennings Hart," Arthur confirmed. "Did you know him or know anyone who knew him? We're friends of his sister and promised her that if we were traveling though the area we would check for her." He lied.

She put her hands on her hips and studied Arthur's face.

"Who's she?" The waitress asked tilting her head in my direction.

"She's my mother." He looked her square in the eyes with his boyish charm and smiled as I kicked him on his shins under the table.

"Now that's true, I thought to myself remembering that Arthur always forgot what he did yesterday. But the kick was justified retaliation for his impertinence. And I didn't know about him, but for me it felt good.

"Jennings' sister is my friend." I fortified his lie with my own.

"You finished?" she asked looking at our empty dishes and without waiting for an answer began to pile plate upon plate until the surface in front of us was clear. "I'll bring you your check."

She quickly turned and walked away with our dishes and our hope of a connection with Jennings. I was beginning to feel a little helpless even though I knew it was only the beginning of our second day in Marienville. Maybe coming here was a mistake. Maybe we were on a journey to nowhere and this whole thing was just a waste of time.

Arthur sensed my despondency and reached over to reassuringly squeeze my hand. The rolls had switched for a moment. He was the consoling parent and I was the child.

Within minutes our young waitress came back. "You can pay at the counter," she said as she placed the bill on our table.

We gathered our jackets and walked to the front of the restaurant where we saw the older waitress taking payment from another customer. "Might as well take care of y'all while I'm here,' she said without recognition of the conversation we had five minutes before.

She quickly processed the check and handed Arthur back his change. "Suppose y'all want this little thing on the bottom as a record." She then tore off the small perforated portion of our bill, gave it back and clicked the register shut without a glance our way. Well, I thought, so much for southern hospitality. She's been up North for too long.

The morning air was beginning to warm up as we walked to our car. "What next?" Arthur said sticking the small receipt in his jacket pocket.

"Let's go to the factory again and take pictures. Just to jog our memories after we leave this place." I suggested.

I felt that once again we had really hit a dead end. The State Police investigator that had worked on the case had retired years ago and the other investigator that could possibly have given us information was on leave. I was beginning to think that my dream to have closure had led us on a wild goose chase. Perhaps I should have let this whole matter lie and die its incomplete death.

21

The factory was just another scene that deepened my sense of futility. The sight was truly depressing. The large building itself was in a complete state of neglect. Weeds were thriving around the structure and in some places growing out of the crumbling mortar between the bricked part of the walls.

The same species were taking over the railroad bed that stretched between the rusty rails that lead from the loading docks to who knows where far in the distance.

The biggest portion of the building was galvanized metal that had broad streaks of rust and corroded areas on the exterior. The glass windows that once were, no longer remained, only the casings survived the vandalism that the empty structure tempted.

The earth tones of the setting rose from the ground and swallowed up the structure and became one with it. The brown, grays and russets of the overall scene dissolved into one another; this man-made structure, dying and becoming part of the earth again. More slowly surely, but in time to disappear and bend to its destiny.

Then within this forlorn sight my eye caught a glimpse of color. Amid the browns and grays of the decaying landscape was a beautiful old pine in all of its green glory against the clear blue spring sky; one beautiful burst of color shining; a beacon of life among this deathly landscape.

"Arthur, come here I have to show you something."

"Here. Look. Right over here. Take a picture of that tree and angle it so you get the building, too."

He took out a tissue from his pocket to wipe the lens of his camera. I saw something fall from his pocket. "Something fell to the ground from your pocket over there. Want me to get it?"

"No, I see it." Arthur bent over and picked up the small white thing and was about to put it again in his pocket when he stopped. "Well, I'll be. Would you look at this? I think we've got something here," he said quickly walking toward me.

"It's the receipt from the restaurant. The one that waitress gave me. Look. Here on the back."

I took the receipt in my hand and saw written in pencil a telephone number and a note to call between 5 and 5:30 tonight. Our southern belle must have written it on there. Maybe she didn't want anyone to hear her talk to us, so this was her way of communicating that she knows something. Or at lease is willing to talk to us.

Our first ray of hope since we arrived. Maybe, just maybe, our luck was turning and we could start putting the pieces of the mystery together somehow. I felt we were on to something. Just what, I didn't know yet, but I felt the darkness beginning to lift.

Just as I was feeling positive, the sound of an approaching car behind us interrupted the quite of the abandoned scene. We turned just as it pulled up beside us andthe driver wound down his window. The man was wearing a dark jacket with a badge pinned high on the left side. I looked quickly to see if it was a Sheriff's car, but it was unmarked. Only a bracket of lights ran across the top of his car.

"This here's private property, folks. Didn't you see the 'No Trespassing' sign posted at the end of the drive there?"

I noticed a slight bulge in his cheek that I hadn't seen since I was a child. My grandpa used to sit and rock, chew tobacco, and periodically with perfect aim, sling its juice into the spittoon beside him. I suspected this guy had the stuff squirreled in his cheek, too.

"Well, no, I didn't see it, but we're just looking. We knew someone who worked here and just were curious." The truth usually served me well.

"Ain't no excuse. See you got a Jersey plate there, but anyone around here who can read knows a 'No Tresspassing" sign and what it means. Suspect you do, too, so do yourself a favor and move on. We don't want anyone getting hurt around here."

"Sure, sorry. Ooh, did you know a man by the name of Jennings Hart?" In spite of, in hindsight, a better judgment of what *not* to ask, I did.

He smoothed back his hair and readjusted his hat. "Don't believe I do," he said and then spat out the window just missing my foot. "Now, next time you see a sign that tells you you're not wanted on the property, you'll know what to do?" He pulled his car in reverse and left.

"I've got icicles in my ears from that smart-ass," Arthur said as we headed off the property. "Do you think he was anyone with any kind of real authority? We were kind of dumb not to ask. We just assumed."

I was just about to say that it really didn't matter when we noticed the man was waiting for us at the end of the road. I gave him a wave as we passed by and headed back toward the main road. So much for mutual trust, I thought. I hoped that we would never see that character again during our stay in Marienville. At least we got some good pictures and I could walk away from the glass plant finally having an image of where Jennings spent his days.

I remembered the plant's logo on the letters Jennings used to send to us and my trying to imagine what this place looked like. The cage where the demon that I feared spent his days. I felt rather ashamed thinking of him that way now. Now that he probably was dead. But back then, my fears and the image were genuine. I could almost picture him in his office with big interior glass windows protecting him from the plant's noise and the world outside of his schizophrenia. Sitting, hunched over his desk, pleading that I love him again. He would write with small precise lettering forming the words and filling the spaces between his mind and the pen.

I never threw his painful letters away. I secured them with a rubber band and tucked them in the back of my dresser drawer. If something happened to me, they would be there, as evidence. Just in case, I used to think as I added them one by one. Just in case Jennings killed me.

We knew the afternoon would drag by slowly in anticipation of our 5 o'clock phone call. We decided to spend the time to find the nearest town that had a public library to see if they kept any microfilm of local newspaper articles. Maybe we could get new leads from other newspaper accounts that I did not already have.

The day before the dispatcher in Tionesta had told us that that Oil City was our best place to start researching, so we figured that was the best place to start.

In my mind the town of Oil City was a dark place, because of its name. But I was pleasantly surprised as we drove past the farms and forests that surround the city and entered onto the main street. Splendid homes set comfortable back from graceful tree-lined streets greeted us. Even in the bare state of early spring, the gray branches mimicked agile ballerinas, arching over the sidewalks. It was certainly a far cry from the rustic area that is nestled between two federally designated Wild and Scenic Rivers in Forest County, where Marienville resides. Forest County has close to fifty percent of its land within part of the Allegheny National Forest. No wonder Marienville seemed like a natural escape for Jennings. I had heard years ago from an uncle who lived in nearby Clarion and worked in the strip mines digging for coal, that the Oil City landscape was reminiscent of an Americana that was quickly disappearing. I could see now how it got that reputation and was surprised that it had been able to remain as it was.

The discovery of oil in 1859 by Colonel Edwin Duke started the famous oil rush. Like Steubenville and its steel mills, people came to Oil City to make money. During 1865 as the town historian proudly notes, approximately half of the oil shipped in the world was shipped out through Oil City. So those who came and worked hard were not disappointed. Many became rich and built the gracious homes along the streets; evidence of the wealth provided by the black gold.

In Oil City we found the library that had sent me the articles that I had asked for before I started on my trip. We parked diagonally in front of the library and climbed the few steps to the entrance. Arthur pulled open on the heavy double doors that wore worn gilded letters indicating that we, indeed, were in the right place. The years of mountain weather and eager hands on the doors had erased much of the library's identity. I wondered if maybe there was a newer library elsewhere, but we were lucky to have found this one. Once inside the building, we were helped by an assistant who eagerly directed us to the newspaper archives.

Why is it that libraries seem to squeak more than any other public structure? Perhaps it is the quiet that makes it seem so. In spite of our caution not to break the quiet decorum, Arthur and I squeaked our way across the wooden floors to the long oak desks. As we slid our chairs from beneath the desk, they scraped and echoed across the expansive room. Even my effort to gently place my bag on the table failed. The result was a resounding thud that bounced of the high walls. I didn't have to question whether my noise had disturbed anyone, because the shuffling and coughing from the annoyed occupants let me know.

I have always believed that libraries are one of the few architectural wonders that allow us to use most of our senses. I sniffed. Smells like an old library, I thought. It was a universally recognized aroma, a mixture of dusty paper and pine oil. The same musty bouquet the big old library in Steubenville had in the morning after a night of mopping the floors. For me, it always had been a comfortable smell. I was solaced that the Oil City Library was as it was.

Unfortunately, we were not there for our own pleasure. I would much rather our visit was to find a great book to take our minds away from all of this unpleasant work. Much better to be here to read one of the best sellers on the New York Times book list, or search for a classic that I would like to revisit. I could think of a thousand other reasons to be here than the task that brought us.

Arthur and I spent hours going through all of the material that we were able to gather, trying to find any speck of new information on Jennings' disappearance. We scanned every microfilm containing reports by the local and county newspapers back in 1980.

All of the pieces more or less covered the facts as they were and as we already knew them. The basic who, what, where and when were covered. We wanted to know why and who 'done it'. That we knew we would *not* find in the library.

Basically, all of the accounts agreed. Jennings got up for work like most residents of Marienville that Monday morning on January 21, 1980 and drove his car to work. His destination was the Marienville Glass plant where he was supervisor of the mould division. He showed up for his shift that day, left the plant a little early and gassed up his car, and that was the last time anyone in Marienville saw him. Jennings had spent the weekend back in

Washington, Pennsylvania with his family and one of his girlfriends, drove back to Marienville and that is the last time anyone back in Washington or here saw him.

All of the articles were the same as the ones that were sent to me by mail weeks before. We were not able to uncover any new evidence or facts in the case by finding additional news stories covering this incidence. Our main concern and probably our only hope at this point, was still the waitress from the restaurant. We hurried back to our motel so that we could make our call in the privacy of our room.

We arrived back at the motel around 4:30 that afternoon. I was nervously pacing the room as Arthur was going over questions we could ask her. We had decided the plan was to try to set up a meeting with her if she really could give us pertinent information. Then there was the chance that the number was another contact other than our waitress. Maybe it was someone else who could give us the information we needed. Whatever would happen as a consequence of that call we wanted to be prepared.

At 5:05 we made the call. I sat on the edge of the bed, hearing only one side of the conversation. I silently prayed that Arthur could convince her to meet with us. He was a good salesman. Certainly if he had been able to convince me to marry him, as afraid as I had become of my marital instincts, he surely would be able to persuade her to meet with us.

I could tell from Arthur's answers that she was still questioning him. Would she please meet with us, on her own terms? Finally, after Arthur told her the truth about us, and who we really were, and why we were asking, she agreed to meet that night at her house. Arthur took down the directions and hung up the phone. "I hope we are not walking into something we can't handle." Unless she was playing some kind of game with us, I was sure she was thinking the same thing from her end.

"We've made the decision to come here, let's have faith that something will protect us. Do you have the feeling that we can trust her?" I asked.

"Yes."

"Okay then, we'll go."

22

Our southern belle's house was about five miles from our motel and with only one wrong turn we finally made it to the edge of the camp where she lived. As we turned up the road we saw a small log cabin on the left with the front light on.

Her instructions were to pull up along side of the cabin and turn left into the gravel drive on the side of the house.

My heart was racing a bit as we knocked on her door. If Arthur was nervous, he hid it well. She quickly opened the door and motioned for us to come in. The room was larger than it appeared from the outside and was very cozy. The center of the room contained a small Franklin stove that rested on a raised brick platform. Her furniture was arranged so that all of the seating benefited from its warmth. Soft colorful pillows accented the couch and chairs and she had plants near the windows that were dressed in soft tieback curtains. A group of framed photographs of faces that I assumed were special to her were on a side table at one end of the couch near where Arthur and I sat.

"Would you like something to drink?" she offered.

"No thanks, we're fine." I replied.

She was much prettier than I had remembered from this morning. In the dim light and in civilian clothes she did have a sort of softness that I didn't notice on our first meeting. She moved to the chair opposite us, and as she passed through the light overhead, I could easily imagine she was very pretty when she was young.

She was the first to speak, "Well, what you told me over the phone, well, who are you, really?"

I didn't know what to expect, but her question caught me off guard. I thought Arthur had explained to her over the phone.

Arthur didn't miss a beat, "As I told you over the phone I'm her husband and this is my wife who used to be married to the man we were asking you about, Jennings Hart. My wife and her children have been living with a ghost that won't die until they find out what happened to him. We're just here asking for help from you or anyone who can shed some light on his disappearance. We just want to know, that's all. Then we'll go away. She just wants answers for herself and her family. If they don't, if they can't, then they will spend the rest of their lives waiting for him. They will never be able to bury his memory until they know. It is as simple as that."

"I thought so,' she said softly, "but I had to be sure. This is a very small town you know. Everybody knows everybody else's business. It's very hard to keep secrets, unless you have certain connections. Then the secret is safe because people are afraid." She nervously brushed her hand along her lap as if to wipe away something too small to see. "You can't be too careful."

She reached for a cigarette, "Smoke?"

"No. Thanks." We replied.

She lit up and inhaled. Held it and let the smoke free from her lungs into the air.

"Should we be afraid?" I asked.

"No, not now." She said.

"How do you know that?"

She was quiet and I could tell she was carefully deciding just how much she was going to tell us.

"Because I was one of his friends. One of his close friends."

"Girlfriend?" Arthur asked what I wanted to.

"Yes. At the time I thought I was his only girlfriend, but in the end, after it all came out there were others."

"Others? How many others?" I asked her.

"At least five around here, maybe others somewhere else, who knows." She looked at me.

"That's okay. We were divorced. He was free to do whatever he liked. Please, go on."

"He was so handsome that one. Could charm a bird right out of a tree. He'd come into the Kelly Bar on Saturday nights, all dressed up. Closest thing to excitement the women in this town had ever seen. He would stroll up to that piano and sing. He could have had any woman in this town he wanted. He was good, real good."

"Did he have any male friends? Like on the job or at the drinking spots?" Arthur questioned. I knew he was searching for a suspect.

"Sure. He had friends. But his stories made some enemies, too."

What kind of stories?" I asked knowing that Jennings probably continued to create stories as he did with me.

"Well, he used to brag a lot about things, just this and that, but it turned some people off. Like the way he could get women and he talked about... Well, just bragged about things. After awhile it was hard to know what was true or not. Even with me, but he was so... Well, I guess I thought he loved me. So I wanted to believe him. Until I knew..." Her voice trailed off.

"About the others?" I added.

"Yes. Well, there was this one. I won't give you her name, but she was married. Jennings used to sing in church and she played the organ there. I guess they became good friends and he would go to her house and practice. After awhile they were more than friends and she started taking up with him on the sly. It was awhile before her husband suspected anything. Then one day she takes off… leaves her husband and goes into hiding. Who knew what was between those two? Everyone in town knew he had this crazy man temper, so everyone suspected she just had it up to here with him and left town. Then her husband found out she had cleaned out their bank account of $50,000. Right away he smelled a rat. Knew something was up. Nothing probably would have come of it if Jennings had kept his mouth shut. But I guess it really wasn't like him, he couldn't help himself."

"What do you mean? What did he do?" I was by now on the edge of the couch afraid of missing one word of her story.

The tip of her cigarette illuminated as she drew on it. It was awhile before she answered.

"He and I had gone out to dinner at the Bucktail. We were sitting at the bar for a drink while waiting for our table and in walks a guy from the plant.

"One of the men working for my husband…."

"Right. But I didn't think anything of it at the time. Most of the men in town stop by often for a drink. As I said before, everybody knows everybody in a town as small as this. Anyway, Jennings is talking to him and bragging that he is going to buy one of the camps outside of town."

'Oh, yea, with what!' the guy laughs. 'Us son-a-bitch mould makers don't make enough to save anything.' The guy then turns away and pokes his friend and winks.

'Oh don't you worry. I've got my hands on $50,000. I think that'll buy that place real easy, now. Don't you?' Jennings says being real cocky."

"Well, I'm just as shocked as the guy is, but I write it off as just a put-down to the guy. Jennings was embarrassed in front of me, so he had to say something I figured."

"You don't say you lucky son-of-a-bitch", the guy says as he slams his drink down on the bar. Then he gets up, takes his friend and leaves. I look over at Jennings, thinking he had gone a little too far with this guy, and he is just sitting there smirking like a little kid who just beat up the town bully. What was that all about, I said to him. His reply to me was, 'Don't you worry your pretty little head about it Sweetie, I just was bustin' his balls.' Just like that he says, he was just bustin' his balls. Between you and me I knew it was a bad thing. Jennings was messing with the wrong people. But I didn't really know how much or I really would have been scared for both of us. After all, I was his girl, or so I thought..."

I looked across at her as she pressed the stub of her cigarette in the ceramic ashtray on the arm of her chair. I felt an air of sadness about her; an emptiness. I pitied her. She obviously loved Jennings. Twenty years ago she would have been my rival, today I could only feel sorry for her and remember the pain.

"I thought I was, too." I heard my voice and stopped. Do I really need to share with this stranger a part of my past that was up to this disclosure, my own?

She looked up and slowly shook her head. "We sure weren't lookin' under the right tree, were we?"

As much as I didn't want to face the truth, I couldn't have said it better myself. Our southern belle was right on target.

Arthur pressed on. "So, what happened after that?"

"Nothing. I mean, he called me late the next day and said he was going to see his kids back in Pittsburgh that weekend and he promised to call me when he got back. I never saw him again."

"Did you try to call him when you didn't hear from him?"

"Yes, but there was no answer. I didn't think too much about it, just thought he may have stayed an extra day. Then on Tuesday I called him at work and when he wasn't there and they hadn't heard from him either, I got mad. I started thinking he should have called me if he was staying longer."

She paused to light another cigarette and waited to take the first draw before she continued. "And then I heard they were looking for him and not even his family knew where he was and I got scared that, well, I don't know what, but that something had happened to him. Well, I knew he wouldn't just go away. He really loved his kids and wouldn't walk away from them. I didn't say anything to anybody, but I knew he had also been carrying a small gun in a shoulder strap. He told me it was for protection out at his cabin. It was isolated and about eight miles from town and this being so rough a part of the country and all. Well, I just believed him… that's all. But when he disappeared I thought maybe the gun was for something or someone he was afraid of."

"When did you find out there were other women in his life?" I asked.

"Everyone knew, after awhile, when the State Police were investigatin' and asking questions everywhere. There were a lot of rumors goin' round and a lot of talk about what happened, but nobody really knows for sure."

"What were the rumors?" I asked.

She brushed her thumb against her chin while her cigarette curled smoke in a thin stream in front of her face and she seemed to leave us for a moment. Moving her hand away from her face to flick her cigarette, she returned. "I have to say the biggest thing going around, talk that is, was that he was in the Mafia or was connected somehow."

"Are you kidding?" I said. "What would make them think that?"

"I don't know. Maybe it was all of his stories, like he was hiding something. Anyway, I'm just tellin' y'all what they were sayin."

"What did you think. Did you think he was in the Mafia?"

"I think he was just a guy who liked to tell stories because it made him feel good," she said.

"It was his way of being somebody," I replied.

"Yes, I think so."

"I guess we all want that, but he just needed it more somehow and tried to get it the wrong way."

"Well, that's really all I know," she said as though to signal the end of our visit.

As she walked us to the door we thanked her for her help and I asked her if she could lead us to anyone who could help us further. I impulsively reached for her hand, invading what privacy she so clearly was holding onto, and I looked into her tired eyes. "Please what is her name? It would help me." She looked surprised but didn't reject my forward gesture, slowly taking my hand and giving it a slight squeeze.

I knew it was difficult for her to expose her life with Jennings anymore that she had already, so I didn't press her further. I knew how she was feeling. I had been there myself. She didn't make any promises, but said she would think about it and call us at the motel if she could recall anyone and started to close her door as we walked toward our car.

"Marie. Her name is Marie Cocumelli." She had called out behind us so softly that I barely heard her. And then she was gone behind her locked door.

Arthur and I drove back to the motel that night feeling as though we had opened the door to our mystery, but we didn't have clue as to what was inside.

We hadn't gone more than a half-mile when a car appeared in our rear view mirror and stayed there long enough for us to consider that maybe we were being followed. I tried not to keep looking back, but the bright lights behind us were steady and did not turn away. I was getting a bit nervous and hoped that the vehicle would turn off some side road before we reached the motel.

Arthur and I rode in silence, each hiding from the other our suspicions about the headlights. Then as we reached our motel and pulled into the lot, we didn't have to wonder anymore. The car pulled in behind us. It was our friend who had sternly ushered us off the factory property the day before.

"Howdy, folks. Now you two sure are 'busy-bees' drivin' these back roads so late at night," he said as he pulled in beside us. "I wouldn't recommend strangers roamin' around in this remote area at dark. Why you folks in town, anyways?" With that he spat out the window. I was feeling grateful that I was safely in the car and out of his firing range this time.

"We just had dinner in town at the Kelly and were driving back here after a short stop," I said, thinking that I did not want to implicate our waitress into our investigation. "Are you the sheriff or something?"

He spat again and I could hear him put his car in gear. "Or something?" he questioned, mocking me. "Food at the diner up in town is right good. Chicken pie is mighty fillin'." He drove on by and left us in his dust wondering whether he was friend or foe.

My sleep that night was restless in anticipation of tomorrow and what might be our last day of discovery before leaving Marienville. I didn't want to go home without an answer.

23

The first thing we did the next day after looking up Marie's address in the local phone book, was to go to the Exxon station and fill up. Arthur got directions to her road, which we soon found out was not that far away and as close as the other side of town.

This possible lead made me more curious than ever before. It went beyond the investigative level into a more personal one. Who was this woman who broke up her marriage at great risk for my ex-husband? Since I now realized that she could have been the catalyst to Jennings' eventual fate, whatever it was, I knew that if we lost the chance to interview her, we would have to work around her. This would be a waste of valuable time cutting to the chase. In addition, maybe lose critical information that would help us solve the alleged crime.

Marie's house was easy to find. It was a nice A frame, a better home than most we had seen in the area. It had a wide front lawn and a distant view of the Allegheny Mountains.

As we drove along I could see that the mountains ahead were also still bare and were not yet greening. They appeared to me as imposing lords, graying at the temples and standing proudly. The sun rose and set behind those proud pinnacles that controlled the light in Marienville while they watched silently over their vast domain. They knew what we didn't. I'm sure they had seen it all. Somewhere within the shadows of those mountains the truth lies. I was certain.

We pulled into the long gravel driveway that had an old Ford truck resting without its wheels on cinder blocks at the end. We parked the car and heading for the front door, we eagerly climbed the wide cement steps leading to a generous porch that ran the length of the house and was made of the same gritty mix.

I rang the doorbell. No one answered. I pushed the button again, allowing what I thought to be a courteous interval to elapse between rings and waited. No one seemed to be at home.

All of this anticipation for nothing, I thought, another disappointment. Then just as we had given up and turned to leave, I heard the door open behind me. I turned around to see standing before us in the doorway, a woman that I very much hoped to be Marie.

"Can I help you?" she said with an annoyed edge to her voice.

"Marie Cocumelli? I asked.

"Yes, that's me. What do you want?" she replied hesitantly, looking me up and down.

Well, there she is, I thought to myself. Finally, we meet the probable femme fatale that inadvertently started this whole mess. Unless she had changed drastically in the past years, she looked nothing like what my movie prone mind would classify as someone who would be cast to steal Jennings' heart. Her overweight body belied that maybe she at one time did have a beautiful figure. And her hair, now mostly gray, showed a few dark brown strands curling through its wiry texture and fell to her shoulders, made her look even more matronly. Perhaps it was unfair for me to assume, but money does make strange bedfellows, I thought, while looking at her.

"Sorry to bother you, but we are relatives of Jennings Hart and we asked someone in town who they thought might know him best. They mentioned you. They said you might be able to help us fill in the pieces of his life before he disappeared," I said trying not to expose my anticipation.

"Don't know who said that, but they're wrong. Can't help you. That was a long time ago. I don't know more than anyone else around here, besides that's the past and I don't see any use going there. I've got a life and what happened to him, who knows? Maybe he just run off or something, who knows?"

I didn't want to lose her, so I was cautious as I pressed her for more information. "We certainly understand that, but just maybe if we could talk awhile, you could remember one thing that would help us … one thing that would seem like nothing to you, but would mean a lot to us."

"Got nothin' to say to you. I already told everything I know to the State Police. Go talk to them. They got everything from everybody. Now you leave 'cause I'm going to say good-bye and shut the door."

And she did, leaving Arthur and I standing there facing the wide oak door with its tarnished knob that now separated us from our big piece of the puzzle.

I'm loosing my edge, my ability to get inside and get answers as I used to do when I was digging for stories at work, I moaned silently to myself as we descended the thick steps toward our car. What could I have done differently to keep her from getting away?

"Well?" I said aloud, looking at my husband.

"Well, what?" Arthur said putting his arm around my shoulder as we walked. "There is no 'well' about it. She didn't want to talk and she wasn't going to talk no matter who she thought we were. If we had been detectives, she would have asked us to speak to her lawyer. This gal is no dummy and she knows the ropes. We struck out because she didn't want to play ball, that's all. Don't beat yourself up over this. Let's move on to something else."

He was right. Arthur knew me better than I know myself and the law of averages, providing we persevered, would assure us another door would open to us sooner or later, I had to believe it. But I had to think, remembering Marie's big chunky steps, that it would have been a great place to hide a body.

It was still early and I decided I wanted to visit the judge that denied issuing a death certificate for Jennings and, although I suspected a deeper motive behind his actions, I thought it wouldn't hurt to see him and plead my case to him once more. There was always a chance I could change his mind.

Dctcrmined not to give up, I made a few more inquiries and found that there were two circuit judges that were working the Forest County area. His address was listed a town twenty miles away from Marienville. Trying not to waste a day of precious time, we hopped in the car resolute in our desire to get an answer about the death certificate issue.

The smell of pine disinfectant was present when we closed the car doors. It's probably still on our shoes, I thought. As we rode along the scent caused my mind to travel to the Saturdays Mother and I scrubbed the house in Steubenville in an effort to erase the truth about our lives.

Unfortunately, after several dead-end phone calls and a visit to the country seat, another door slammed in our faces when I discovered that he had retired and gone south somewhere.

Arthur and I looked for the road that would lead us to the judge's house. His place was easy to find. One of our less difficult trips yet, I thought as we pulled up the long driveway to his house that rested comfortably in the middle of a small grassy rise. The manicured colonial brick structure was larger than the other homes on the road. The judge must have had a solid career before he retired.

Two rings of the door chimes that softly heralded our presence brought an elderly woman to the door. "Is your husband in?" I asked politely assuming that she was the judge's wife.

"What is the nature of your business?" she replied, her knarled arthitic hand clutching the edge of the door, seemingly protecting what might be behind the threshold.

I really did not know how to respond. I knew why we were there, but I didn't want to assume her husband was the one responsible for blocking my receipt of a death certificate. At least until we knew the whole story and had the facts, not just my intuition.

"We're from out of town and are looking for someone who is familiar with the circuit judicial system in this area."

"My husband isn't very well and isn't accepting visitors. You might try the court house in the county seat," she said. “I'm sorry we can't help you.”

Perhaps it was my active paranoia that had been somewhat heightened during our investigation here, but I thought I saw a man's shadow move across the hall behind her just before she closed the door. The shadow was wearing a cap similar to that of our tobacco chewing friend back in Marienville.

"I may be crazy, Arthur, but I think that man who has been following us is in that house."

"Come on. How could that be? We’re miles away from Marienville. And how would he know we were coming here, anyway?"

"He could still be following us, that's how."

"I don't know. Let's not run away with ourselves here. We have focus on Jennings and that end of the mystery."

"I'm sorry. You're right. We have enough to think about without complicating things. Right now we should get back to our leads on Jennings. Let's head back toward the motel."

I certainly hoped that this was not an ominous sign of what the day's end would bring for us as sunset was approaching and we headed back to our motel for the night.

Feeling at this point I had nothing to lose, when we approached a camp and I saw a man chopping wood outside the main cabin by the road, I told Arthur to pull in.

Who knows, maybe this guy could help us. It's such a small place, knit within the mountains, maybe he knows something about Jennings. By now I had hit so many walls, I was grasping for straws. What did I have to lose but a little time?

As we parked and stepped out onto the dusty ground near the man, he eyed us suspiciously and resumed chopping. It was as though we were invisible and all attempts to get his attention were ignored. He totally rejected any overtures on our part to be friendly.

Then just as we had given up hope and were about to turn away, the sun now set firmly behind the mountains inhibiting us from seeing clearly, a tall figure stepped out of the shadows of his cabin doorway. He slowly moved toward us, the crimson glow of his lighted cigarette, a beacon smaller that a cat's eye, marking his forward path.

"You askin' 'bout Hart?"

His words, spoken in bass tones that seemed to emanate from deep within his chest, were music to my ears.

"Yes. Did you know him?" I asked as he approached, giving us a better view of him in the cabin's light. His lean muscular torso was supported by long legs that slightly bowed at the knee and were wrapped in tight faded jeans that hung on hips, loosely held by a large silver buckle that shimmered as he walked. In spite of the chilly evening, he wore only an undershirt, exposing a large tattoo of some kind of bird on his right arm. Whether is was from my anticipation or my absorbing his cold, I don't know, but a slight shiver went through my body as he reached us.

"Might say… you relatives?"

"Well, yes. We're trying to piece together what happened to him and so far haven't had much luck," I replied, figuring I might as well be a honest as I could be, hoping against all hope he wasn't just yanking us around.

He stopped in front of us and cautiously took his time looking first at Arthur and then at me. Taking a long draw of his cigarette, then turning his head in the direction of the oblivious 'wood chopper', he released the smoke in his direction. "Don't mind him. He got too close to a double barrel when he was no higher than a squirrel. Can't hear a damn thing. Don't talk neither, just chops away all day long like some crazy fuck! Come on in an we'll jaw a bit," he said indicating the direction of his cabin.

Arthur and I looked at each other feeling we had nothing to lose. After several days in Marienville were still nearly at ground zero in our investigation, so we decided following this man into his cabin, although a little risky, involved getting the information we needed to push forward.

Once inside the sparsely furnished cabin, he cleared his dinner plate from the table and motioned for us to sit down and to take a seat on the couch near the wood stove that warmed the room.

"I wasn't exactly expecting company, just finished supper. How 'bout a cup of coffee," he said as he poured us cups of coffee from a battered pot warming on top of the stove. He stoked the fires in the already warm cabin and poured himself a cup. With one strong arm he swung his chair around, the rungs facing us, and in one smooth move he straddled the chair with his long denim-covered legs. Sitting forward, his bare arms resting on the back rungs, he began his story. His worn face and furrowed brow accented his words as the information we so eagerly had been hungry for was spun together in a dark tapestry before us.

I was a bit nervous both in anticipation of what we might learn, as well as being behind a closed door with a tattooed stranger.

"Why you wanna' know 'bout Hart?" he said looking directly at Arthur.

Arthur gave him the same information we had given the waitress about my quest for answers to my ex-husband's disappearance. Repeating that it was a personal mission and nothing else and ensuring him any information he could help us with would make our jobs a lot easier.

"Your husband, he was a good lookin' dude, I'll say that for 'em. Could sing, too. Damn. He was good and the ladies swarmed all over 'em like flies when he'd sing them tunes of his at Kelly's. But he was stupid. He had a big mouth and it finally got him in trouble. Don't really know what happened to him, but I can tell you what I do know. I got this buddy, see, and one day he comes to me and asks me to drive him in my truck to see some friends of his who come from out'a town. He said his Ford was laid up in the garage and he needed to see these guys before they left town. Now my friend was goin' through hard times with his wife. She left him for another guy he thinks, anyway, they's separated. He was walkin' 'round with a long puss all the time, so when he said he needed a ride to Joe's Motel, just a piece south toward Clarion, I say, why not? So I take my friend and when we get there, he tells me to wait in the car. Now, bein' his friend and all, I thought that kinda' strange, but I do what he says and I wait in the car figuring I'll smoke a butt or two 'till he comes out. Now he gets outa' the car and walks right to the room without havin' to even ask the room number to the cute little gal at the desk. In less than I can smoke one cigarette, he comes back out, doesn't say nothin' and I drive him back home. Now he gets outa' the car and leans thorough the winda' and says, 'This trip never happened.' The next day your husband was missing and my friend is walkin' around with a smile on his face. When the State Police came to me I told them my story and said I wouldn't go no further with it or testify or some shit like that. Excuse me ma'm, but I'd rather rot in jail than be a dead man, if you know what I mean."

"Why are you telling us this now?" I questioned. If he had been so afraid to testify, then why be so free with strangers. I didn't understand that if he was telling us the truth, why now, especially to people just off the street. I was curious as to why he was willing to tell his story to us with the chance we could go to the authorities with the information.

"Doesn't matter now, you'll find out soon enough. I ain't afraid no more. Simple as that," he said.

"I'm afraid I don't quite understand."

" Get yourself to the county records office and figure it out. That's all I can say."

"Can you give me your friend's name?" I knew I was treading in dangerous territory.

He just looked at us and remained silent for what seemed like eternity. Then he got up and slid his chair back under the table on the side of the small room and lit another cigarette.

From what we could gather from this fellow's story he firmly believed his friend had arranged for the Mafia hit on Jennings, because the next day after the motel meeting Jennings disappeared, without a trace, from the face of the earth. End of story.

I sat there, staring into my empty coffee cup, feeling as though someone had just punched me in the stomach. If this man was telling the truth, then Jennings not only was dead, but more than likely suffered a horrible death at the hand of a man vent on retribution. I could only imagine what tortures were designed and executed to make Jennings suffer for his indiscretions with the wrong woman.

"That's all I know good folks. I've gone as far as I am gonna go, the rest us up to you. Nice talkin' to ya. Need directions outta' here?" he said showing us to the door.

He had to be talking about Marie's husband. It was just a guess, but I felt I was right. Everything else fit. The separation; Jennings' bragging; the old Ford truck that I saw in Marie's driveway, it all kind of came together. The Mafia puzzle and the motel visit. Everything sort of fit. Maybe Marie's husband had a hit put on Jennings to make him go away forever. We had so many loose ends and yet nothing to tie it together.

Maybe I should have been leery about this stranger, after all he only gave us what he wanted, only part of the story, but I had a feeling he was honest with us. I don't know why, but I guess it was just my gut instinct that made me trust him.

If I was right, then we could cross check his story. I would have to think about that one. Maybe after I had enough time to digest everything we had so far, maybe after a good night's sleep, tomorrow I would know what steps to take from here. At least I knew, if all that had come forth as of now was true, we were close to putting together our puzzle.

On the way home I kept thinking, wondering why he was no longer afraid to hide his information about the 'friend' that I suspected was really Rocco. What in his life had changed that would take away his fear?

Was he dying of some terminal disease that made his fate already chosen? What was it? That question kept going over and over in my mind, even as I lay in bed later that night, my active imagination delaying sleep as I restlessly tossed and turned.

Eventually I dozed off, but then suddenly in the middle of the night I awakened with a start. My subconscious mind must had been on overdrive as I slept, because it finally hit me, I thought I had found the answer.

What took away my fear of Jennings, my fear of being killed by him? Of course, it was so obvious. Death. Death brought me freedom from fear. Rocco was dead. That is why the fear was gone from our campsite friend. Rocco was no longer around to retaliate. He told us. We had to search the records; the death certificates, obituaries, anything that could verify that my supposition was correct. Tomorrow we would begin the search.

24

The first thing I did the next morning was to call my old friend and investigator, David Fuhry, in Pittsburgh to start scouting for information about Rocco, including looking into the possibility that he had relocated to Youngstown. Then Arthur and I scoured for the next week every county record and newspaper microfilm in all of the adjacent counties we could uncover. Unfortunately, we dredged up no documentation that would lead us to suspect that Rocco was no longer with us.

The only information we found about Rocco that anchored my position that he had Jennings killed, and also gave me an indication of how volatile Rocco could be, were several newspaper clips and court documents indicating that Rocco had once allegedly threatened someone with a gun. The case was dropped and dismissed when the plaintiff didn't show.

The same judge that denied me a death certificate for Jennings was the judge that dismissed the case against Rocco. But because I don't know all of the facts, it was a supposition. Quite possibly it was pure fiction.

Having hit an information wall and my eyes bleary from the voluminous stacks of records I had been sifting though for days, we thought it might be a good diversion to have a nice meal and turn in early so that we could get started again at sunrise. We headed once again down the road facing our unsolved puzzle.

Certainly I believed it was one of the judges on that circuit in 1980. One of them helped derail any paperwork that would finalize Jennings' disappearance and allow a death certificate to be written. My guess it was the judge that we visited. Shadow in the hall or no shadow, my famous gut told me so. But the reality was that the law was not based on my intestinal instincts. I had to dig further.

Even in the darkness the roads around Marienville were becoming so familiar to us that by now we could drive them by rote. As we navigated the final stretch into town our lights cut though the thick duskiness ahead. We both were tired and rode silently, each in our own thoughts.

Somehow part of the darkness started to lift. We became aware of a car approaching us from the rear with the bright lights reflecting and blinding us in our rear view mirror. Arthur reached up to flip it to night viewing when suddenly the car sped past, lurching into our lane. Arthur swerved over into the berm just barely missing a tree and came to rest after running over some dry brush. It happened too fast for us to see what kind of car it was, but I was convinced it was no accident. Whoever it was didn't want to kill us, or they would have run us off the road in a section that didn't have such a level berm. I believed it was a warning. Someone out there wanted us to go home and stop snooping. Where could we get help? Whom could we trust?

That night, both of us exhausted by the stress, I fell into a deep, deep sleep and I didn't wake up until noon.

"Honey, wake up. I've locked myself out." It was Arthur. I looked at my watch. Twelve o'clock! How could I have slept so late?

"Okay, I'm coming. I'm awake." I swung my legs out of bed, my middle-aged muscles still stiff from a stressful sleep, and opened the door.

"I went to get coffee and forgot my key. I tried to get you on the phone and it has been busy for 20 minutes. At first I thought you were talking to the kids, but then the motel clerk said it seemed that the phone was off the hook."

Arthur moved toward the phone. "Aah, he was right. You must have knocked it off without noticing it. Didn't you hear it buzz?"

"I had a restless sleep last night, but I sure didn't hear any buzzing. Sorry."

"No. It's just that our waitress friend called the motel this morning and made a connection for us with someone she think can help us. I took the call at the desk. Apparently he was privy to the whole investigation. He has retired and doesn't live here anymore. She wouldn't give me his name or number because this fellow wants to remain anonymous, so we have to wait for his call."

"When did she say?"

"Around seven this evening."

"That's good news. I thought she was finished with us didn't you? By the way, I take back every nasty thought I had about her in the restaurant. So far, she has been our only savior in this town."

"I'm anxious to get out of here, aren't you? If this man can tell us anything new, I'm all for packing it up and going home. I'm beginning to believe we are never really going to know the truth about what happened to Jennings. This could turn out to be an eternal quest, you know."

"At least we're trying, Arthur. How about instead of hanging around all day waiting for his call, be go back and see if anyone else was with the ambulance crew other than the guy in North Carolina."

I finished dressing and Arthur and I grabbed something to eat in town and went back to Kelly's to see if

Joe had anyone else with him when they were first investigating Jennings' disappearance.

There was an older man behind the bar that was almost empty, except for what I assumed were regulars who were waiting before the doors even opened each morning.

I looked around and noticed the woman who had been tending bar the day we arrived in town. She had just hung up the phone near the kitchen doors. "Hey, glad you came by. Didn't ever think I would see you again. After you left and I thought about it awhile and talked to some folks around here I found out Whitey Stiles was down at that missing guy's house when they were going through things. He works across the street at the Exxon."

We thanked her and walked across the road to the same Exxon station we got our gas the other day. After asking for Whitey we were pointed to the garage where a car was hoisted in a lift that two mechanics were fixing.

"Whitey Stiles?"

"Yup. What can I do for you?"

Again Arthur explained our mission and that we would like to talk to him because we understand he might be able to give us some background on what he saw.

Whitey wiped his hands with a greasy rag he had in the back pocket of his overalls and showed us to a small back office. "Coffee?" he said pointing to the machine against the wall.

"No thanks. We're fine." I said.

"You're Jennings' wife?"

"Well, his ex-wife, actually. I'm here to get just to get some answers for my family and myself. That's just about it. I've heard stories, but haven't been able to talk to anyone who was really there when they found out about him and started looking."

"Don't know if I can add anythin' you don't know, but I can tell you at least what I seen. Jesus, you mean they never know yet what happened to him? It's been years now and we ain't heard nothing, but I thought maybe they found him and we jus' never heard."

"No. That's why we're here," Arthur said.

"Where you want me to start?"

"You choose. How about when you arrived at the house?"

"It was four days before we knew he was missing."

"Four days!" I couldn't believe that so much time had elapsed.

"Yup. That's right, four days. And when we all got there it was another two days after that. By the time we all got there, people already had been walking through the house, cleaning and disturbing things. I never seen anything like it. The troopers were all put out because there was nothin' like a crime scene left. It had snowed and the ground was not the same. They did find change, nickels and quarters and things between the garage and his house. Might have been a fight or something. But the dogs were out there sniffing, but there was not much to go on. His car was there all gassed up and his suitcase still on the table, but not much else. Rumors were goin' round he had Mafia connections, but don't know if it's true. Joe and I stayed awhile, just curious, but we brought the ambulance back to the garage, 'cause there was no use us hangin' around without a body."

"That's something we hadn't heard before. About the struggle, I mean. Did any of his neighbors hear anything do you know?"

"I heard that his neighbor at the time who lived up the road heard a truck go by with a V-8 engine. Ford, I believe," he added.

"How could anyone tell the make of a truck just by his hearing it go down the road?"

"Well, this neighbor was special. He was a musician and earned his living by tuning instruments for all the bands in the area. He knew his sounds and he said it was a Ford alright."

Very interesting, I thought. Maybe, if that neighbor is still around, we could speak to him and verify what Whitey has told us.

Not having much more to add to the puzzle, we thanked Whitey for his time and he gave us directions to the musician's house. Seems we were in for more luck. He still was around.

We headed back down the road to Route 899, retracing the route we had driven the first day toward Jennings' house. At the Virgin Mary statue we turned down the rough road and at a small log cabin, the house nearest to Jennings' old place, we pulled into the musician's driveway, hoping we would find him there.

We saw a vintage Chevy station wagon in the driveway, its back window plastered with stickers from all sorts of places its owner must have traveled, so we thought we might just get lucky and find someone at home.

A floppy-eared hound pup met us at the end of the driveway and was anything but a watchdog. He playfully barked and pulled at Arthur's cuffs as though he was chasing rabbits that kept slipping from his tiny teeth with Arthur's every step.

As we approached the stoop a lazy old Basset hound, his legs so short his ears barely missed scraping along the moist grass glistening with dew, came around the house and warned his master of our presence with his deep resonant bark. The noise prompted the front screen door to open, and there stood the man with graying hair pulled back in a ponytail that we hoped was our musician.

After calling his frisky pup to his side, he stood on the stoop and the old hound disappeared back around the house. We explained for what seemed like the thousandth time, why we were there and he indicated he would be glad to tell us what he knew. He invited us inside and encouraged the puppy back out the screen door to find other things to chase.

The basset's master was a man in his fifties with a neatly trimmed graying beard that seemed to have a hint of red to it, much more than his hair that was as best as I can describe, the color of graying wet sand.

I looked around the large room, cluttered with phonograph records and all types of musical instruments, some in cases laid about; others on the large table on the side of the room.

The walls of his cottage were of knotty pine that had darkened with age, and at the back of the large room was a bay window with a worn leather seat at the base that was strewn with more vinyl records in their worn sleeves. Guitars and other string instruments filled corners of the room in stands and a zephyr on another small table in the center of the room. An old upright piano was on the far wall with sheet music piled high on the top. This indeed was a house of music, I thought.

I knew my son would drink in every inch of this room if he were here, knowing every record and every instrument and the craftsman. But for me it was an oddity and insight on a way of life of an artist who surrounds himself with his creativity and has little need for anything else but the basic comforts; food, a roof over his head and his dog.

"Are you a musician, or do you collect?" I asked pointing to the guitar on the chair in the far corner.

"Yes, both, but this is not all my stuff. That guitar there is, but I tune guitars, violins, all kinds of instruments for the bands around here. There are enough here 'abouts, so it keeps me kind'a busy."

"My son's a musician...singer, too. He has an old Gibson he just loves."

"This here is a Gibson, real old one." he said picking up the instrument and lovingly stroking the honey-colored neck before he placed it carefully back to its resting-place. "Great guitar. Belongs to a friend of mine."

He cleared off the couch, scattered with newspapers and books, so that we could sit.

We talked with the musician about Jennings and the night he heard the Ford with the V-8 engine go past his house and a short time later return in the opposite direction away from Jennings' house. Since he is gifted with perfect pitch there was no doubt in his mind he was accurate about that.

As far as he was concerned, he said, "Hart more or less was a loner, like so many who come up here to live in these parts. Never heard much going on over there, though. Just time to time, his quartering wood, you know, splitting it… the sounds of the hatchet clicking against the wedge. Always sounded kind'a musical to me… the rhythm and all."

"Were you home the day Jennings supposedly disappeared?" I asked to see if Whitey's version of the story was true.

"I was. And one thing kind'a stuck out in my mind that I told them."

"What was that?"

"About sometime late that afternoon I heard a Ford V-8 truck go down the road toward Hart's house," he said again. " A little later I heard it come by and head out toward 899."

So, he had told the authorities what he had heard and told us that he hadn't known Jennings' well. Just from time to time they would pass on the road, or he would hear the sounds traveling to his house of wood being split. He knew it was his neighbor adding to the growing pile next to his house.

Checkmate. I looked over at Arthur to see if he had heard what I had. That piece of the puzzle clanging loudly into place.

"Did you see it? Did you look out of the window and see it?" asked Arthur.

"No. Didn't have to."

"Why? How did you know it was a ford V8 if you didn't see it?'

"I've got perfect pitch and I know a Ford V8 when I hear one," he said proudly. "Everyone 'round here knows that."

We then stayed awhile talking with him about my son and his music and dogs and other things people talk about when they feel a thread of commonality connecting them. It was the first time since we had arrived in Marienville, that I didn't feel like a square peg in a round hole. He expressed sorrow at our loss and appreciation of our pride in our musical son. We shared our respect for his craft, our love of dogs, and our thanks for his willingness to help the investigators years ago.

I left the musician's house feeling that the puzzle was now nearing completion, knowing we were on the right track. Maybe not yet at our destination, but definitely moving in the right direction, and definitely motivated and determined to find the whereabouts of Rocco Cocomelli. We were almost certain in our minds Jennings did not just walk off into the horizon. He had been murdered and we had learned who was responsible for killing him. Now if the next phone call we were expecting this night tied it all together, Arthur and I could go home with some kind of conclusion to the case.

I was a little nervous thinking that this anticipated call was really our last chance to find more about what happened to Jennings before we left Marienville. It would be very frustrating for me not to be able to find some definite answers, after all these years, once and for all.

25

We ate dinner for what we hoped would be our last night in Marienville. We drove to the small diner on Main Street. It wasn't crowded at all. The early risers were probably at home now getting ready for their television shows. After an early start to their day and before they hit the bars later on after dinner, the town seemed relatively quiet.

"Look at how much we have learned up here," Arthur said, while slicing into the freshly steamed trout on his plate, "I kind of understand Jennings a little bit more now that I've put him in this atmosphere, seeing the kind of life he chose to be in. I can't say I'm much like him in that respect, but there is a certain sense of raw adventure up here. Sort of on the edge of civilized life. Not quite in, yet not quite out either."

He was right, and our southern belle was right, also. Everybody did seem to know everyone else in this town. There must be a certain comfort in that. Being able to go out and be somewhere where they actually know your name and the names of your wife and kids. To be able to walk down the street and know there will be someone there to give you a smile of recognition. I have lived in urban areas so long that I had forgotten how nice that is. There is a certain comfort that if you are missing or in trouble someone will miss your presence and know it.

But I honestly didn't know how I felt. I would just be relieved to get this whole thing over. Talking to the waitress especially shook me up a bit. I kind of saw pieces of myself in her and it was depressing for me to look at myself so honestly through her eyes.

After dinner we arrived back at the motel and waited for our contact to call us. I had dug down to the pith, the final truths as we know them, and now all we could do is wait to see if what we will learn will complete Jennings' tragic story.

"Is he calling here?" In my rush that morning I had forgotten to ask.

"No. I gave him the number of your cell phone. He doesn't want to chance anyone from the motel hearing the conversation."

"What would you have done if I didn't have a cellular phone?" I wondered aloud.

"Pay phone in town," he replied.

I'm beginning to feel like we are hiding from the Mafia."

"Maybe we are."

"Now that's a comforting thought. Don't say that."

I got up and went to the motel window, pulling back the lined drapes that closed out the sunset. As I looked out at the row of weathered cabins across the road, the melancholy remains of a way of life, the smoky beams of the soft alabaster sunset filtered through our room. I retraced in my mind the days we had spent there and the people we had met. I realized I would be taking away from there a piece of my ex-husband that I hadn't had before; memories I could not erase.

I had a new sense of him in his surroundings; his house; where he ate his meals; his friends; his lovers; his enemies. And now I had also had grievous slices, segments severed and sewn together forming a tragic scenario that I must now relay to my children.

My daughters still had their father, but for Lee, this was it. The final word. The final page with his father.

Two minutes after seven my cell phone rang. I crossed my fingers like I used to do when I was a little girl and wanted my wish to come true.

"Hello," my voice was trembling with excitement.

The caller responded. "I trust Dixie, she said you're both who you say you are."

So, that's her name, I thought. The caller had unknowingly opened up information to us that our southern belle had not wished to share so willingly days before.

"Just exactly what is it that you want from me," the caller asked. I recognized a strong local accent. He must be from this area.

"I just want to know whatever you can tell us about what happened to my husband, Jennings Hart. Dixie said you might be able to help us. Can you?"

"Well, I don't know if it will help any. Not much you can do with what I'm going to tell you except just take it in and leave it there. If that is what you want, then maybe I can."

"That's all," I reassured. "All I want is to be able to make some sense of my husband's disappearance."

"Now I wasn't there at the beginning, but Jennings was to meet with one of his girlfriends the night of his disappearance and he never showed. Well, I was told she then went to his house looking for him and when she couldn't find him, she called his family back in Pittsburgh and found out he had come back to his house on Sunday. That made his family worried and when he didn't show up for work the next day, they high tailed it up to his house looking for him. They came up and looked around. They went in and they cleaned the house. Four days after…ahh… like on Thursday, they called the State Police barracks."

I couldn't believe that I heard that they had waited four whole days. That confirmed Whitey's story, too.

"Right. And when I got there it was another two days beyond that. In the meantime then, there had been like ten or fifteen people out at the house walking around."

"Putting fingerprints all over?"

"Yup. Cleaning the house, moving things. There wasn't anything like a viable crime scene, really, by the time I got down there and got involved in it."

"I can't understand that because my sister-in-law called me in New Jersey to see if I had seen him. You know, because he had a habit of stalking me. He would come up and hide behind the bushes and sit in his car outside of the house because of his paranoia. Even after I got the divorce from him in 1977, he would still follow me around from time to time. So they called me to see if he had come up in the area and maybe I had see him around, but I hadn't. But I thought maybe someone had reported him missing right away to the police or, ah, the State Police and then maybe they went right to the scene of the crime. Evidently the whole situation was moved around because too many people were there and too many things had been disturbed for them to see whether of not there had been a robbery or.."

"Yea, uh huh. The only thing that I had after a short time, I had gotten a metal detector. I went down and there was snow on the ground... uh…for several weeks there around the time of the disappearance. It snowed that afternoon as a matter of fact and I figured that anything that was outside would be covered. I took the metal detector and went around between the garage and the house there and I recovered. I think it was 36 cents in change that indicated to me that there had possibly been a struggle or something. Or he could have been reaching into his pocket for his keys and someone might have accosted him at that time or something like that. The only other thing I found that was even nearly out of the ordinary around the house was the fact that there were come coins laying in the yard between the driveway and the house, but that it is out of the ordinary is stretching it a bit."

"But you never found his car keys or anything?"

"No. There were a set of car keys, but the house keys and things like that, seems to me, if I can recall now, like I said the house had been entered. Gone through and I'm not sure if there was a set of house keys or not."

"His wallet or nothing like that?"

"I can't recall exactly where the keys and everything went to. I don't think there was a set."

"I wonder why people would have gone into the house, though, and looked through things. Were they trying to find something that would lead them to…" I asked.

"Yea, I think they were looking for, ah, Jennings was supposed to have had a diary. And I bet you some of these people were looking to see if they were in that diary. See that's just a supposition on my part."

"Maybe."

"Just a supposition because the diary allegedly was never found. I'm not even sure it existed. I have a little book here with some numbers and some names and stuff like that in it, but I didn't really have a diary or anything like that. But, well-meaning people who cleaned up a little bit and things like that."

I shook my head, "I'm not too sure I agree. No. Because in just the last couple of years my son… We've all blocked this out because it is so painful. But my son said that he remembered one time when his dad came outside our house in maybe 1979 or maybe '80 he did notice he was carrying a gun under his jacket. He was afraid to tell me because Jennings had been violent before and the police had to come to our house and take away his rifles and ammunition. There was a period when he was so normal and then he would just snap and be another personality. I think Lee had blocked this out until recently."

"Now I now think that maybe it is because someone had threatened him," he added.

"Well", I continued, "I find it very curious, because Jennings did have a history of being institutionalized for mental problems, and how someone like him could get a permit to carry a gun."

"He probably didn't have one. There was no indication of Jennings having a permit in Forrest County Court House. But back in those days you get a permit in any county in the state. It was valid in every county. I did check Harrisburg and I don't think there was a registry on file for him there either."

"He may of just had one..."

"... Illegal one?"

"I found that strange, too, because during our life together he had rifles, but never any handguns or would ever think of carrying any kind of firearm. That kind of makes me suspect also that he was in trouble of some kind, or else someone had threatened him. Otherwise, why would he carry a gun on him?" I added.

"Yea. Most people don't do that unless they are afraid of something."

"Is it true that he was dating someone whose husband had connections with the Youngstown Mafia? I asked.

"Well, ah, yea. That was where I leaned two ways on this investigation. I had discovered that Jennings had prior mental condition and had been treated for paranoid schizophrenia and I had in my mind possibly that for some reason he had taken off. But that the only reason that that was, was because of his history. But his car...he had filled up his car with gas up at the Exxon station that afternoon around three o'clock. His car was setting in his driveway.

So if he had planned on taking off, he wasn't going to fill up with gas and let it set."

"I agree."

"But there was a... the Cocumelli lady, the one that was having the problems with her husband. Ah, Jennings had gone over to their home and he sang while Marie played the organ and things like that. Now Rocco, her husband, he remarked, I interviewed him several times, that he didn't like the way Jennings and his wife looked at each other and talked and this and that. Rocco was the guy, I did a lot of background on him and he used to live in Pittsburgh doing numbers. He had some connection with the Mafia in Cleveland and Youngstown."

"That's scary." I said

"Well, when Marie left him in the end of December there, she withdrew fifty-thousand dollars from their joint checking account and this was of some concern to Rocco. He was pretty upset about that. About that time I was told that, ah, Jennings like to jack people around a bit."

"Yes, he did." How well I remembered.

"He was heard making the remark that he was thinking of buying the Gateway Lodge. He had a fifty-thousand-dollar down payment. Very shortly after that, well, within a couple days after that, Jennings made the remark on a Thursday and on Friday, I think he went down around his Pittsburgh girlfriend's place and stayed Saturday and Sunday. He came back, went to work Monday and when he got off work, just disappeared. But he had allegedly made that remark and it got back to Rocco. So I think that he had the impression that Jennings was going to be spending his money."

"That doesn't surprise me one bit," I said. "Jennings was very persuasive and so charismatic that women would do almost anything he asked. Trust me. I'm living proof. Even women that were intelligent and should know better. No one was immune to his charms. Except maybe Rocco."

"Well, Marie. I talked to her several times and she told me, "I didn't give him the money and that money had nothing to do with me and Jennings."

"Somehow I don't believe that. It seems very suspicious. Who would take that large amount of money out of the bank? Did you ever find out what she did with the money?"

"Well, they got their divorce and everything was finalized and settled and the couple… She just moved out, didn't have any income or anything like that and she just drained the bank account and took off. Disappeared. She was just kind of protecting herself, really."

"I see. But did she really disappear?" I questioned.

"Marie?"

"Yes."

"No. She just disappeared from Rocco."

"Oh. I see what you mean."

"I knew where she was. I kept in touch with her and I talked to her. She said, you know, there was a good possibility, but she didn't think her husband was involved, and so I had made arrangements with her for a phone tap, and I had some questions, 'cause Rocco…she gave him her phone number, but she did not give him her location, you know…"

"Uh huh."

"I made arrangements for a phone tap, but the petition to have it was turned down, so I couldn't wire tap their conversations. But I wanted to get into Rocco. I went after him a couple of ways and then I got a call from his attorney advising me to quit harassing his client or I'd be liable for a civil suit. Once they invoke the attorney privilege. That's it. You really can't go after them then. In fact, for a few months Rocco was off limits according to the statutes."

"Well," I thought, " that's too bad because it does seem. I mean nobody is guilty until proven, but it seems that maybe he didn't do it himself. I mean, if he had connections, wouldn't it have been easier to have it done for him?"

"I came across a fellow in Marienville that I had heard was a friend of Rocco's and had spent a lot of time with him. Particularly when he was going through this separation. Rocco was just about beside himself with anger and frustration and everything else. For about a couple of months there, especially when that money turned up missing. And the weekend that the money turned up missing, Rocco approached this fellow in Marienville and said, "I need a ride down to Joe's Motel." That's about fifteen miles south of Marienville, down by Clarion. And the guy took Rocco down to the motel. Allegedly, Rocco got out of the vehicle and told the other guy to wait and he walked to a room without going to the front desk. He knew which room to go to. He walked up to a room at the motel, went inside, met with two guys. Within ten or fifteen minutes came back out and told the man to take him back to Marienville. He said, "This trip never happened." The guy is convinced that Rocco had contracted somebody in the Mafia and he had arranged for Jennings..."

"For a hit?" I interjected.

"To be taken care of. Now I tried every way I could to get this guy to present that testimony to a grand jury, because I wanted to indite Rocco without even having a body. But, ah, the guy told me, he says, 'I will go to jail before I will say that to a grand jury.' "

The stranger we met at the camp was telling the truth. That must have been him we spoke with the other night on our way back from Marie's. I'm sure at the time he was afraid for his life.

"He said, 'I value my own life, my business. I'd rather be in jail for a year than to have to be worried about these guys for the rest of my life.' And well, I'll tell you what. About a year later I came across another investigation and I had this same guy for something else and I offered him immunity if he would testify and he had the same answer."

I wondered if the man still lived in town and that he was the same man we talked to in his cabin, but my caller continued before I could ask.

"In my investigation I interviewed Jennings' neighbor that lived about a quarter of a mile up the road. Now this guy said he remembered hearing a Ford V8 truck go down the road the day around 3:15 the afternoon Jennings supposedly disappeared. I questioned this guy as to how he could tell it was a Ford V8 and he told me that he had prefect pitch and he could tell this motor from others. For years he made a living tuning guitars and other instruments for all the bands and musicians in the area with his perfect pitch. He said he had no doubt. Well, he didn't know what I knew. Rocco was the owner of a Ford V8 truck. Seems everywhere I turned the fingers pointed to Rocco's involvement in the investigation."

"It's like beating your head against a brick wall," I said.

"Yea, over and over again. Jennings had at least three girlfriends in or near Marienville and the only connection I could go with was his alleged connection with Marie. Rocco and Marie had a nice A frame and Rocco was putting in some cement steps in the front and I put a lean on him and said, 'Listen, I'll tear up those steps unless you tell me what happened to Jennings.' That's when I got the call from his attorney."

I remembered the remark I had made to Arthur about those chunky steps at Marie's. Was it prophetic or just a coincidence that this man and I would think the same thoughts about those steps? "You said you did a background check on him. What else did you learn if anything about him?"

"Nothing other than what I told you, but I did know him from before this all happened, and I was aware that he had quite a hot head on him. Rocco's camp had been robbed along with several other camps in the area. We caught the two guys that did most of the robberies, but they did not confess to robbing Rocco's. So Rocco took it upon himself to get his gun and confront the guys. He went to their cabin and kicked in the door and held them at gunpoint, put the gun into the roof of one of the fellow's mouth, trying to force a confession out of him. Luckily for the two guys, Rocco had a more levelheaded friend with him who convinced him to cool off and let the law handle them. Well, it winds up that these two guys didn't do it and we found the ones who robbed Rocco. At least one innocent man could have had his head blown off, if Rocco hadn't been stopped."

"No wonder Marie left. Her life with him must have been terrific. Any man other than what she had probably looked good to her. How old was Rocco?"

"About sixty-two at the time, if I remember correctly."

"Then by now he'd be about eighty-three or four?"

"If he is even still alive," he added.

I asked if Rocco was still around in the area.

"No. He gave his house to Maire. It was a pretty nice place, too. He moved to Youngstown."

"And Marie? What about her?"

"She's still around, I hear. I talked to her from time to time, but that was it. She more or less made a life for herself. She was forty-eight at the time this all happened."

"So, if I understand what you have told me, you think Jennings is definitely dead?"

"If you are asking my professional opinion, yes. There is no doubt whatsoever in my mind."

"He just didn't walk away into oblivion?"

"No." he replied.

“I don’t think so either. Although I have waited for him for a lot of years, hoping my fears of him could be erased with a kinder sort in my memories,” I said wistfully. “And before we end this conversation, there is another thing I would like to ask you, if you know. Why haven’t I been able to get a death certificate from the state? For years I have tried, but to no avail. I was hoping you could shed some light on that for me.”

"I don’t see why. Back a few years after this all happened, I remember going to court with Jennings’ children by his first wife and testified that I was convinced that he had met with foul play and was dead. It was for insurance purposed that his children went to court.”

My stomach turned. That’s great, I thought, no one even bothered to contact me so that his youngest son could have shared in the benefits and government support through school since Jennings did serve in Korea. Not that he needs it now, but it would have helped us in many ways. It would have been nice for him to at least to be acknowledged and aware of what was going on with his father.

I have tried for years to get an official death certificate, but always got the run around from attorneys, so I finally gave up. Somehow it would have helped just to have an official document that would finalize it all for us.

“I checked this morning and Jennings’ case is still listed as a missing person case. It is kind of remote that anyone will be trying to pursue the case again or go after Rocco. As I said before, who knows if he is still alive.
Well, as one of the young fellows said to me the other day, a good quotation would fit in here nicely, I’m sure, about puttin’ our efforts on a more grand scale, but I’m fresh out.”

I understood what he meant, but I had to get to this level before I could go on to other things. And with that final thought, I thanked him and said goodbye. I guessed that I had to be satisfied with what we now know and go on with our lives. Nothing else could be done in Marienville. There were not too many pieces of the puzzle left to put in place. And it looked like the biggest piece that was missing would *never* be able to be put in place. Where is Jennings and what was done with his body?

Having as much knowledge as I now had about Jennings' supposed murder, I didn't feel safe staying around Marienville longer than I had to. Arthur and I knew too much. If Rocco was still alive or anyone else who had firsthand knowledge of his disappearance was around, our lives could be in danger. Certainly there were enough subtle and not so subtle warnings since our arrival to sent that message. We decided to go home. I was no longer thinking about our vigillante friend in his unmarked car, either. The source on the other end of the phone solved that mystery for us. Our tobacco chewing friend had been just that; a self-appointed keeper of the kingdom from all strangers. He had served in Vietnam and came home a changed young man. He no longer loved to hunt and fish, or work a steady job at the Marienville Glass Plant. His job was to protect his town. I wasn't too convinced he was as harmless as I was lead to believe, but leaving town would take him and his watchdog behavior out of my mind.

After years of trying not to think about my life with Jennings and his death, I thought that if and when I made the decision to validate my pain and let go of the anger that there would be a great emotional healing that would release me. That there would be a great catharsis that would set me free.

So then why was I sitting there trying to fight back not tears of joy, but tears of emptiness. Why was there no feeling of an end for me? An end to my life with him; a severing of the cord once and for all. By all accounts, he had been murdered. He was gone and I could now go on with my life.

But as I sat there I knew that there would be no end for me, and no end for my children. How could I have not seen it before? Knowledge gives us power, but it would never give us complete closure; not even a certified piece of paper declaring him dead. It is impossible, because we cannot erase the days Jennings spent as part of our lives. The memories of those days and years we will carry with us forever.

So I have traveled this long journey to discover that in the end to find answers is only part of the closure. But it is not the most important in the trilogy of finding peace within. It is the confronting of truths and the forgiveness of trespasses against us that brings final peace and closure.

That was it. Those were the pieces of my life I was looking for. That was my closure.

I remember reaching over to squeeze Arthur's hand. Our places were set in life as husband and wife. We communicated with our silence as we sat side by side that spring evening at our motel in Marienville. Words were not necessary. We both knew. The best of Jennings lives through his son. The best has survived.

I don't remember too much of our trip back home, but I do recall that the next morning as Arthur pulled the car out onto the road and we headed back to New York, I lay back against the headrest and let my tears come. Tears of joy and freedom. I knew that Jennings had freed me. I had been released and my new journey was just beginning. I couldn't wait to see what was around the next bend in the road.

26

When I got back, I called and wrote letters to every state and county office in my search for a Death Certificate for Rocco. The process was painstakingly laborious. Request after request, inquiry after inquiry, and no luck. Having had researched to dead ends, I finally came to my senses and decided that I had to close my notes on my past once and for all and start writing my story. What facts I had would be the best I could do. That was easier said than done.

I began writing about my findings in 1996 and it took me many trips back to Marienville, Pennsylvania and many interviews and days of investigation to finalize my quest for closure and what actually happened to Jennings.

Sometimes the efforts and discoveries became so painful that I would have to stop and put the investigation aside for awhile. One time I stopped for a complete year. But then, my drive for the truth would pull me back and I would start again. The hardest part in writing about something so close and so personally painful is that it has a tendency to creep into one's current life.

Besides, enough is enough. As an actress and journalist, I also know what can happen when a character's life almost overcomes one's own being. I know how difficult it is to remain in character, or at the typewriter for months at a time. To be able to let go of work when I walk off the set or close my office door and go home to my regular life each night is a challenge if I remain deep into a project, whatever it may be. The crossover is so strong and such a pulling force that it sometimes is impossible to separate what is real and what is not in my present life.

One immense positive of my husband's schizophrenia is my determination to expose this illness as an affliction that should not be hidden. It is my opinion that schizophrenia should be celebrated. Not as in 'honored', but as in 'widely known'. We should not be reluctant to admit that this disease exists in all social strata; all peoples of varying nationalities and races. It knows no boundaries. Schizophrenia knows no prejudices.

Jennings was a brilliant, if troubled, man. He was an inventor. He had an accomplished musical talent. His intellect was sharp. But his reality was blurred by his schizophrenia. There have been great minds, creative talents and Nobel Laureates that have suffered from this form of mental illness. It can attack all ranges of intellect from the bottom to the top of the scale. Without a doubt, uncontrolled, it is a dangerous and debilitating illness. But there is hope on the horizon. With ongoing research and medical advances available today, early diagnosis and proper medication can often make the disease manageable and allow the patient to live a more constructive life.

As for my perspective through all of this, I have discovered that where I have been is as important as where I am going. I am no longer looking back, but I acknowledge my life as I have lived it. I may not have wished it, but I am grateful for the challenged path I have walked, because every step of the way has made me a more compassionate human being. As far as I'm concerned, that is a great place to continue walking forward.

AFTERWARDS

It was with great trepidation that I dared to let any of my life turn into a manuscript. I still carried the heavy baggage of the pain and embarrassment of the things that happened years ago. Realizing that my words would be a revealing picture of who I am, or was, and perhaps laying my soul too bare, I was not confident I was ready to share my life's journey beyond the confines of my own soul.

It was not until I began work with NARSAD, National Alliance for Research on Schizophrenia and Depression, a national not-for-profit organization whose primary objective is to raise funds to find the causes, cures, better treatments, and prevention of the severe mental illnesses, that I realized that my story was important. If this organization, founded more than ten years ago by family members and professionals who are convinced than a better future can be found through expanded brain research, could devote their lives to helping those like Jennings, then I should not be so selfish and hold back what I had most to share. If my experience with my husband could open one person's eyes or could save one life, then I had to speak out. Along with NARSAD, I had to try to bring schizophrenia out from behind closed doors and into the main stream of awareness. If anything, something positive had to come from Jennings' life and our pain.

Fortunately, The children and I have weathered the storm of living with mental illness as well as can be expected. Arthur and I are living on the New Jersey Shore in the house Jennings and I bought thirty years ago, and where I raised my three children. I still am enjoying the ocean view and writing about my life, past and present. In the end, when I look at my years on an overall scale, life has been good because I have acknowledged my past mistakes.

Brett, my oldest daughter and her family live close by and they are an ever-present and wonderful part of my life. She is a creative wonder and is an inspiration that constantly gives me fodder for my pen. My first grandchild, Marshell, is my best friend and we often talk as friends do and walk the beach together discovering treasures left from the early morning tides.

Alison still loves horses and she and her wonderful Irish husband have a horse farm in Lexington with lush green pastures as far as the eye can see with neat white fencing monitoring their silken equine inhabitants. Little Billy, just under two, has beautiful wide eyes that don't miss a trick and soft blond curls that I love to nuzzle against my chin when I hold him. He is faster than a jack rabbit and gives his Nana a workout when she lucky enough to be in his presence.

My son finally found a soul mate that loves him and understands where he comes from. He is making his life count by giving back to the world something meaningful through his music. His father is still mentioned in his lyrics from time to time, evidence of haunting images and memories of a man he hardly knew. His first album won a Billboard Award in 1997, and he continues to create music from his heart that touches ours.

I couldn't be a more proud mother. Each child has walked through our dysfunctional family life as whole as can be expected, and each is giving back to society in a positive way. The scars may still be there, but they have chosen to look forward to the future, and not let the past cloud their positive outlook on life.

And the most surprising and pleasing aspect of my life today, where I am at this moment, is that *Behind The Magic Mirror* has been embraced and has been an inspiration to many who have lived with mental illness. Since the embryo of the book was to be solely a catharsis for me, this happening is one of the biggest bonuses in my life, and I am grateful.

Someone asked me that if I had to live my life over again, would I change anything. It was quite a question, one that I suppose we have all been asked at one time or another. I didn't have to blink and eye when I replied that I would probably not change anything, except perhaps, for not recognizing Jennings' schizophrenia earlier in our marriage. Maybe it would have saved his life if I could have detected the nuances that would have alerted me to his illness before it got out of control and into the acute stages

What Grandma said to me those many years ago while lovingly plaiting my curly head, I am grateful to be able to finally recognize. I have learned to appreciate the good in my life that for awhile, seemed very hopeless. So what if my plan is not the one that life has mapped out for me, I can't complain. So far, to say the least, it has been a very interesting trip.

Paths

I am but a thread unraveled and trailing from the hem of
His celestial robe.
The length of which can glow in finite dust stirred by
the Infinite motions of His mantle.

I am free to choose the path by following my dreams
Gathering, Absorbing, while traveling in
the footsteps of my Higher Power.

I am free to relinquish the path, lingering at the wayside
Struggling, Agonizing the journey while caught by the
Thorns,
Severing my soul's source of Nourishment.

Where appropriate, names and characters have been altered to protect the identity of those who cooperated in the investigation of Jennings Hart's disappearance and to protect the innocent.

1. Opening of Romper Room, Bert Claster Enterprises©
2.To My Children, (1989) Sandra Hart©
3. The Gift of Life (1977) Sandra Hart©
4. Paths (1982) Sandra Hart©

Mental Health Resources

National Mental Health Association, 1021 Prince Street, Alexandria, VA
22314-2971 (http://www.nmha.org)
Information Center 1-800-969-NMHA
NAMI/NYC, 432 Park Avenue South, Suite 710, New York, NY 10016
(http://www.nami-nyc-metro.org)
NARSAD, 60 Cutter Mill Road, Suite 404, Great Neck, NY 11021
(http://www.mhsource.com/narsad.html) 1-800-829-8289
Open The Doors - Schizophrenia
(http://www.openthedoors.com)